Thomas Hardy

FEMINIST READINGS / SERIES EDITOR: SUE ROE

Thomas Hardy

PATRICIA INGHAM

HUMANITIES PRESS INTERNATIONAL, INC.
Atlantic Highlands, NJ

First published in 1990 by Humanities Press International,
Inc., Atlantic Highlands, NJ 07716

© Patricia Ingham, 1990

Library of Congress Cataloging-in-Publication Data

Ingham, Patricia.
   Thomas Hardy   / by Patricia Ingham.
     p.   cm. — (Feminist readings)
   Bibliography: p.
   Includes index.
   ISBN 0–391–03554–1. — ISBN 0–391–03555–X (pbk.)
   1. Hardy, Thomas, 1840–1928—Political and social
views.
   2. Hardy, Thomas, 1840–1928—Characters—Women.
   3. Feminism and literature—England.   4. Women in
literature.   I. Title.
   II. Series.
   PR4757 F44I54   1990
   823'.8—dc20   89–35113
                                              CIP

Printed in Great Britain

Feminist Readings

Series Editor: Sue Roe

The *Feminist Readings* series has been designed to investigate the link between literary writing and feminist reading by surveying the key works of English Literature by male authors from new feminist perspectives.

Working from a position which accepts that the notion of gender difference embraces interrelationship and reciprocity as well as opposition, each contributor to the series takes on the challenge of reassessing the problems inherent in confronting a 'phallocentric' literary canon, by investigating the processes involved in the translation of gender difference into the themes and structures of the literary text.

Each volume surveys briefly the development of feminist literary criticism and the broader questions of feminism which have been brought to bear on this practice – from the initial identification of 'phallocentrism', through the tendency of early feminist critics to read literature as a sociological document, to feminist criticism's current capacity to realign the discoveries of a wide range of disciplines in order to reassess theories of gender difference. The tendency of the feminist critic to elevate texts written by women and the notion that it might be possible to identify an autonomous tradition of 'women's writing' can offer a range of challenges to current feminist criticism, and the key texts by male authors surveyed by the series are considered in this light.

Can there be a politics of feminist criticism? How might a theory of sexual difference be seen to be directly applicable to critical practice? The series as a whole represents a comprehensive survey of the development of various theories of gender difference and, by assessing their applicability to the writing of the most influential male writers of the literary tradition, offers a broad revisionary interpretation of feminist critical practice.

For Sam

Louise DeSalvo	*Nathaniel Hawthorne*
Bonnie Kime Scott	*James Joyce*
Julia Briggs	*Shakespeare*
Jacqueline Di Salvo	*Milton*
Sandra Gilbert	*T.S. Eliot*
Patricia Ingham	*Thomas Hardy*
Kate McLuskie	*Renaissance Dramatists*
Jill Mann	*Geoffrey Chaucer*
Marion Shaw	*Alfred Lord Tennyson*
Margarita Stocker	*Marvell*

Contents

Acknowledgements

I should like to thank Penny Boumelha for enabling me to write this book; Vicky Linklater for helping to check it; Sheila Parsons and Judith Micklem for typing it. I am also indebted to Michael Millgate for generous information about Hardy's copy of Egerton's *Keynotes*; and to Sue Roe for encouragement at all stages.

Hardy References

For all but three novels I have used the first impression of the New Wessex editions (some subsequent impressions have different pagination). For *An Indiscretion in the Life of an Heiress* I cite Terry Coleman's edition (Hutchinson: London, 1976); for *The Woodlanders* and *Tess of the D'Urbervilles* I use the Clarendon editions. The serial version of *The Well-Beloved* is cited from the *Illustrated London News* 1 October to 17 December 1892. *Letters* are quoted from R.L. Purdy and M. Millgate, *The Collected Letters of Thomas Hardy*, 7 vols (Oxford University Press: Oxford 1978–88). The *Early Life* refers to F.E. Hardy, *The Early Life of Thomas Hardy: 1840–1891*, and *Later Years* to *The Later Years of Thomas Hardy: 1892–1928* (Macmillan: London, 1928 and 1930).

CHAPTER ONE

A Survey of Feminist Readings of Hardy

Hardy's novels, almost invariably woman-centred, have proved fertile ground for feminist critics (and fellow-travellers) writing since the 1960s. They present him confusingly as half-enchanted by women's superiority, sadistically disposed towards them or, of course, ambivalent in his attitude. By examining a selection of such critical views it is fairly easy to demonstrate that one reason for this inconsistency is the shifting standpoint taken by feminists over this period, although the now standard account of historical stages is a simplification and an archaeological model is more relevant. Even recent critics incorporate 'earlier' positions, none of which seem to occur in an unmodified form.

What is often excavated as the original position of modern feminist critics is illustrated by Kate Millett's *Sexual Politics* (Millett, 1970) which regards androcentric literature, including the nineteenth century novel, as one more sphere in which women are oppressed by a glorification of a particular set of power-structured relationships between women and men. These, the 'politics' of the book's title, victimise both the women in the text and those who read it. This kind of criticism obviously moves freely between the historical and the fictional, assuming a primitive reflectionism and by implication a reality prior to the novel. A modified but essentially similar approach is still sometimes taken as late as 1982 in, for instance, a representative article by Wittenberg dealing with the central women in *Desperate Remedies* and *Tess of the d'Urbervilles*. Although she allows that 'at the surface level, Hardy's exploration in *Desperate Remedies*

1

of the psychological complexities and the socio-economic difficulties of women is remarkable' (Wittenberg, 1982, p.47), this is seen to conceal only a more insidious oppression. True, Wittenberg admits, Cytherea's sexist lover, Springrove, is implicitly criticised by the narrative as unlikely to offer 'the full-fledged regard and intellectual equality she obviously desires'. But 'another, if less visible, controlling male figure . . . the Hardyan narrator' keeps the heroine in her (subordinate) place by 'intrusive generalisations about women . . . most of which seem condescendingly designed to reduce the struggles of Cytherea and other female characters to the stereotypically female and thus to undermine the reader's regard for them as individuals' (*ibid*. p.53). These generalisations are said to be portents of

> The manipulative, even faintly sadistic narrative stance that would undermine his most splendid portrayal of a woman in difficulty – Tess Durbyfield. Hardy's compassionate recognition and effective dramatisation of women's psychological and socio-economic quest for autonomy is subtly contraverted by a covert need, revealed by aspects of his narrative method, to control and, not infrequently, to punish them. (*Ibid*. p.54.)

The implications of this account are two: that the fiction reflects an anterior reality, in this case patriarchal, and that the male author by creating such a story re-oppresses his heroines and his female readers simultaneously by a fictional acting out of the power-game. The punitive instrument operating on both Cytherea and Tess is the plot, manifested in 'unlikely' behaviour which, presumably, in Tess's case results in her death by hanging. This idea of plot as punishment recurs frequently and unexpectedly in an otherwise critically subtle treatment which declares that 'Tess' circumstances and sexual vulnerability are respectfully and knowledgeably treated as well as almost sadistically enjoyed' (Childers, 1981, p.320). Even if plot is here seen to stop (a little) short of sadism it is none the less regarded as volitional on the part of the author–narrator, a conclusion to be examined in a later chapter.

This begs another vital and neglected question about the status of plots and their authority in a way that requires consideration of Millett's deliberately political equation of narrator and male author. Though it does so less obtrusively by presenting a 'Hardyan narrator' as plot source, it remains critically untenable, given the general recognition of the narrator as a creature of the fictional text and plot as 'nontextual given' (Culler, 1981, p.171). Yet from a feminist point of view it does not matter whether the sexist male is Thomas Hardy or merely the teller of the story. It is not essential to the political argument to identify specific oppressors by name; enough surely to label their fictions sexist.

This first type of criticism merges with what is assumed to be chronologically the next, the kind that attacks androcentric literature for presenting stereotypical women: images of them conforming to the patterns exemplified in Patmore's poem 'The Angel in the House' and the Fallen Woman (earlier Mary and Eve). Kathleen Rogers, who has dealt wittily and at length with *The Troublesome Helpmate*, takes this line with Hardy in an article printed in 1975 (Rogers, 1975). Like the last critic dealt with she modifies her condemnation by allowing that his view of women is 'humane and enlightened' (*ibid*. p.257), but she too raises the issue of 'glib antifeminist generalizations'. She finds that though they are less evident in the novels after *Far from the Madding Crowd*, even *Jude the Obscure*, Hardy's last novel, still presents 'the traditional mysogynistic stereotypes: that woman exploits deserving men . . . that she is . . . an incomplete male'; and that only men 'can rise to an altruism that extends beyond their family . . . [and] combine stability and moral soundness with the ability to think' (*ibid*. p.258).

Such analysis involves the idea that images of women are defective in that they fail to provide role-models for autonomous or would-be autonomous women. Practically and politically it has been necessary to alter women's self-images and men's images of them. Millett's book worked like that, but critically such accounts invite demolition since they are based on unsound assumptions about the literary work. They waver between reflectionism and a plea for didacticism that suggests the demands of early twentieth century 'socialist realism' in art. The unease sometimes surfaces, as when Patricia Stubbs complains that Hardy, despite his efforts to portray 'real women' such as Tess, fails to condemn her virtues of 'self-effacement and humility', which leave her 'defenceless and vulnerable to sexual exploitation' (Stubbs, 1979, pp.82 and 83). Stubbs here seems to be asking for a simultaneous how-it-is and how-it-should-be, as well as making the familiar (and politically unnecessary) equation of male author and narrator.

At the same time this images-of-women criticism involves the question of authentic reflection of women's experiences. This investigation has become a practice in its own right taking various forms, some more subtle than others. Rosalind Miles in 1979 sounds happily Ruskinian about it in relation to Hardy:

> For Hardy the female was his starting point and the summit of his highest endeavour, his initial inspiration and his ultimate goal. In the long search of his lifetime Hardy kept alive a sense of essential elusive woman, the repository of something ineffably delicate and frail, the novelist's own soul dreaming upon impossible fulfilment. This dream of woman was a value that a sensitive man could know, but never be. This essential woman embodies a value that men can recognize, but can never, even the best of them, attain to. (Miles in A. Smith, 1979, p.44.)

Concern to test the 'fidelity' of the text for women in this way elsewhere led readily on to the study by the 'gynocritics' of what women writers had done, not relevant here. In other forms it led in a different direction as critics began to find in Hardy's writing the (desired) feminine. Most deftly Elaine Showalter sees him as one who 'infiltrated' 'feminine fictions' and *The Mayor of Casterbridge* as a demonstration of the fact that he understood the feminine self as 'the estranged and essential complement of the male self' (Kramer, 1979, p.101). The force of her account lies in the skill with which she reveals in the text a dichotomy in Henchard, depending on an original total absence of the skills that he 'struggles finally to learn': those of 'observation, attention, sensitivity, and compassion' (*ibid*. p.114). Her labelling of these as 'feminine', given their obvious human value, makes a forceful political tactic. But it is poor strategy long-term, since it falls in at least with an essentialist view of women to which I shall return and which is fairly traditional.

Her conclusion too is suspect: that the novel is like this 'because Hardy dares so fully to acknowledge this side of his own art, to pursue the feminine spirit in his man of character' (*ibid*.

p.114). Where Wittenberg retreated behind the equivocation of a Hardyan narrator, Showalter expands on the narrator as Hardy by following him into the street. By creating Henchard, she asserts, he swerved 'from the bluff virility of the Rabelais Club, and the misogyny of Gosse, towards his own insistent and original exploration of human motivation' (*ibid*. p.114).

By now it is clear that the critical method of these feminist readings, judged even by such modest criteria as how they handle authorial authority and intention, the idea of 'realism' and the status of plot allow the wrongful assumption that critical rigour is gendered, the preserve of the male. As I hope to show, however, feminist readings can be rigorously supported. It is also evident that the most problematic issue (and rightly) is how 'woman', 'women' (or recently 'gender'), is to be comprehended, defined, constituted, described, analysed. A fairly recent verbal tidying up that gives 'female' a biological and 'feminine' a cultural sense is part of a wider argument. This uses as an analogy the Saussurean concept of 'difference' in language, which describes the value of units in a system in a relational way. Meaningful units of sound in a natural language, 'phonemes', illustrate the fact that in language it is contrast that is crucial and there are 'no positive terms' (Harris, 1983, p.118). Transferring this neutral term 'difference' to gender in critical writing does away with the two possible hierarchies (the less common illustrated by the quotation from Miles above). It also empties the terms 'masculine' and 'feminine' of preconceptions and prejudices about their 'proper' meaning, allowing ideally for a consideration of the two, not only in biological terms but in historical, socio-economic, cultural and psycho-analytical ones as well. Such a concept is useful in keeping a perspective on texts of any period.

Showalter, for instance, proves on examination to be ambiguous about the 'feminine' as observant, sensitive and compassionate in a way which sounds very like the supposedly biologically grounded virtues approved by, say, Ruskin or Herbert Spencer. Such essentialism, if present, always wins a pyrrhic victory because while neither side is likely to deny that women have such qualities, such agreement makes it impossible to get out of the Ruskinian cul-de-sac.

The most sophisticated writer on Hardy's women, Penny

Boumelha, offers her perspective in a way which is critically detached, despite her own commitment to the feminist cause (Boumelha, 1982). She is concerned to look at the historical and cultural context in nineteenth century terms: the ideologies which formed women and the sign 'woman'; and it is in her tracks that I wish to follow. What we are both concerned with is an understanding of the meaning of 'woman' and the statements made about 'her' in Hardy's novels by the multiple voices of the texts.

My account of feminist readings began with the suggestion that their pluralism arose in part from a historically shifting viewpoint whose progression has not been linear; but that is not the whole explanation. Hardy's novels, which extended over at least twenty-four years from 1871 to 1895–7, are not unitary either. Even the circumstances of publication differ enormously. *Desperate Remedies* was produced as a result of advice from Meredith to write a novel with a plot, after Hardy's failure to find a publisher for his earlier work, *The Poor Man and the Lady*. Its plot is elaborate and lurid, involving bigamy and murder. It was printed in an edition of 500 copies and Hardy had to contribute to the cost of publication. When *Jude* appeared in volume form in 1895 Hardy was an established literary figure and though the work produced enormous hostility this was combined with enormous acclaim, resulting in the sale of 20,000 copies by February 1896. The different pressures (external and internalised) exerted in 1871 and 1895 might crudely be expected to produce inconsistency. No unitary account covers all his novels and it is possible to see some plausibility in all the critics cited above depending on where you drill for oil in the novels used as evidence, except that drilling is the wrong way to proceed. The expectation of a consistent account, treatment, analysis of woman/women/the feminine is not sustainable; there is development and doubling-back over the whole span, and even within single novels.

What most of these feminist readings have in common, however, is at least a minimal sense of disjunction, variously explained. It is this recurrence of a fault-line in Hardy that is a crucial link between them: a recognition that in his novels, unlike those of Dickens, Thackeray and Trollope, there is in relation to women a subtle subterranean shifting taking place. It is this that I wish to discuss in certain crucial novels, describing the works before *The Mayor of Casterbridge* (1886) as early and *The Woodlanders*, *Tess*, *Jude* and *The Well-Beloved* as late, in order to do so. Since it is not sound critical practice, I shall not relate them to authorial intention, however gauged, but to the historical context that produces them, including the context of Hardy the man. It is usual to illustrate this kind of approach by a comparison with the way one decodes advertisements in a consumerist society and identifies the meaning (signified) attaching to the signifier *sports car* or *blonde* from a knowledge of the values already attached to them in advertising language. The signs can be straightforwardly used or abused, challenged or transformed, but no speaker starts with a vacuum; to an extent the language thinks him. With nineteenth-century novels it is also true that a particular narrative language exists (as one of several) when Hardy begins to write, already there with signs and the necessary syntax of patterns for narrative sentences as sequences. I hope to characterise the language in order to consider his particular development of it.

This approach also involves the idea that 'the subject' of a novel (in this case usually a female subject) is created by the language, which in turn is a product of ideologies. So it is a construct of the text, a point at which voices intersect, a process which because of its nature opens up the possibility of change. In Hardy's early novels this creation of a subject by the narrative as a whole is somewhat disturbed by contradictions which do in fact show both female and male subjects consciously moving towards new perceptions. Women begin, occasionally, to experience themselves as different from the models accepted by themselves as well as others, with a sense of enhanced, not diminished, self. In the later novels this struggle for autonomy is more extensive and more explicitly articulated. As a result, from *The Woodlanders* onwards, men's perceptions of women as signs become erratic as they try to fit what they encounter into familiar patterns: women seem at times not womanly and yet not unwomanly. A new and problematic space develops in this part of the semantic field which is tentatively and varyingly mapped by each sex. The disruption of the traditional fictional interlocking of gender is increased by the different rates of progress made in recognising it by the men and women involved. This achronology causes tragedy for the individual and, ultimately, the splintering of novelistic form.

There seems to me no sound reason, in considering Hardy's novels, not to consider the whole text in so far as it is available, with all its revisions and rewritings. Theoretically, at the moment, revisions which predate the last edition authorised by Hardy are, with rare exceptions, marginalised and given the status of curiosities. But once the criterion of authorial intention is abandoned there seems to be no logic in this; all versions of the texts are of equal interest. Since I am arguing for the novels, and particularly the last few, as texts in which an evolution in narrative language can be observed, to ignore changes made from one version of the text to another seems perverse. I shall therefore abandon it and use revisions freely, particularly in Chapter 5, making use of the material in the Clarendon editions.

In the transition from early to late novels, discussed in Chapter 4, it is possible to identify a process whereby the meaning of certain signs for the oppressed male (lower-middle-class men and artists) begin to overlap with that of 'woman'. This possibly idiosyncratic equation is crucial to some of the new meaning attaching to Grace, Tess and Sue dealt with in Chapter 5. The last novel, *The Well-Beloved* (more exactly described as a double text), stands in a unique relationship to the other works. In my last chapter I shall attempt to describe this as the metatext reflecting on earlier texts that I believe it to be, which figures in terms of alternative plots Hardy's final views on sexual difference.

CHAPTER TWO

Women as Signs in the Early Novels

At the outset of his literary career, waiting anxiously for the return of his first manuscript, Hardy wrote on 10 September 1868 to the publishers, Macmillan, that he almost felt he did not care what happened to his book 'so long as something happens'. He further asked: 'Would you mind suggesting the sort of story you think I could do best, or any literary work I should do well to go upon?' (Millgate, 1982, p.113). As this shows, it was the mainstream of nineteenth century fiction that he wished to enter. Later events suggest that personal as well as financial reasons dictated this: even when he achieved huge sales with *Jude the Obscure* and could write as he chose, he still internalised critical strictures enough to retain minor bowdlerisings in the volume edition, contrary to his stated intention just after composition. And in the successful novels of writers like Dickens and Trollope, literary stereotypes of women had already been established as simplifications of the complex and contradictory ideals of womanhood found in late eighteenth century women's writing.

The positive side of these simplifications is described by Poovey in her account of images of women in this period:

> As embodiments of the pure ideals of the middle classes, they were celebrated during the nineteenth century for their superiority to all worldly desires. Depicted as a being completely without sexual desire and delicate to the point of frailty, urged not only to be dependent but to cultivate and display that dependence, the Victorian Angel of the House was to be absolutely free from all corrupting knowledge

9

of the material – and materialistic – world . . . the miracle of one who . . . finds supreme self-fulfillment in absolute self-denial. (Poovey, 1984, pp.34–5.)

Two points are to be made about this ideal. It was a reading of legal reality which transposed married women's non-existence (each as a feme covert), non-control of their own property and absence of a right to legal custody of children into a freedom from materialistic taint. Social negatives were encoded as positives. Secondly, the intuitiveness that replaced male rationality as the foundation of the Angel's qualities could be encoded in the dynamic exchanges of narrative in less flattering forms, fed by traditional misogyny. Women can be angelically intuitive or intuitively capricious, wilfully silly; both the angel and the ninny are part of the same essentialist signification of 'woman'.

The question that is addressed in this chapter, however, is not how novelistic images relate to reality but how they relate to the context of which they form a part. The answer is that they encode this two-sided image of 'woman' as sign that was already projected by discussions from the early nineteenth century onwards in books, articles and reviews. This debate purported to embrace a questioning of the image but it presented women as a problem, not as problematic. The terms of the problem were provided by the reactionaries: what was the nature of woman, what were her duties? By implication there were unitary answers to both questions. Those celebrating (rather than justifying) the ideal relied on general assertions of rag-bag origin – religious, aesthetic, practical.

Inferiority is first 'established' by dogma: 'The social subordination of woman to man is a law of nature.' (*North British Review*, 1851, p.518.) Its consequences follow naturally: 'Equality is the mightiest of humbugs – there is no such thing in existence; and the idea of opening the professions and occupations and governments of men to women, seems to us the vainest . . . of chimeras.' (*Blackwood's Edinburgh Magazine*, 1858, p.145.) Crucial structural symmetry is then assumed: 'The more a man fulfils his sphere . . . the more does he become peculiarly a man; and so it is with woman.' (*North British Review*, 1851, p.516.) The subjection of 'woman' is achieved by firmly delimiting her 'natural' sphere: 'To her by nature is allotted the power first of forming and afterwards of inevitably influencing the minds of men.' (*Ibid*. p.530.) And then her exit is blocked on grounds that are simultaneously theoretical and practical – her place is perfectly adapted to her nature: 'Womanhood is purer by native right than manhood.' (*Blackwood's Edinburgh Magazine*, 1858, p.154.)

In the discussion alternative views often appeared, like women themselves, entrapped: they occur usually as limited questions set in an unalterable framework of facts about the duties of prospective wife and mother. So on the subject of education: 'Can anything . . . be more perfectly absurd than to suppose that the care and perpetual solicitude which a mother feels for her children, depends upon her ignorance of Greek and mathematics?' (Revd S. Smith, quoted in *Westminster Review*, 1841, p.27.) And similarly with those women who desire to assume a role in politics the basic theology is first accepted: 'Not one of the reasons given against female politicians can apply . . . [because] the peculiar duties of women are guarded by instincts and feelings far more powerful than the desire of political power.' (*Ibid*. p.48.) Thus the 'woman problem' was tamed in literary discussions; polemics held it in suspense. Sometimes the polemical weapon effectively trivialised the issues, as in *The Saturday Review*'s running discussion of 'The Girl of the Period' in 1868. This offered only the false options of either the 'fair young English girl' of 'innate purity and dignity . . . neither bold in bearing nor masculine in mind . . . a tender mother, an industrious housekeeper, a judicious mistress' (Helsinger, 1983, vol.1, p.108), or 'the Girl of the Period', marked by 'loud and rampant modernization, with her false red hair and painted skin, talking slang as glibly as a man, and by preference leading the conversation to doubtful subjects' (*ibid*. p.112). This trivialisation predetermines the issues in the ensuing debate in the periodical's columns and elsewhere, bypassing the real concern of reformers with the vote, employment, higher education and women's legal status. The phrase itself (often shortened brightly to GOP) became a linguistic model for many facetious and some reductive variations such as 'The Cigar of the Period', 'Puffs of the Period', 'The Waist of the Period', 'The Ordinary Muttonchop of the Period'. The consumerist imagery then as now was an inescapable trap.

Such arguments contained, by appearing to consider, critiques of the womanly ideal; they refurbished and fed, even more than the pious debate, the stereotype handed on as literary currency in mainstream fiction. In choosing to write such 'popular' novels and centring them on women, Hardy was taking up a novelistic language already highly constrained, partly by this continuing discussion. The constraints were also externally (though unevenly) held in place by the circulating libraries like Mudie's which would not lend novels that breached the linguistic conventions. These consisted centrally of a restricted set of 'feminine' signs clustered round 'the womanly' and 'womanhood' and the generic 'woman', a narrative syntax falling into limited patterns, cast resolutely in the indicative (the mood of assertion and definition) and a delimited semantic range that excluded the erotic.

The internal safeguard and measure of these restraints was the required inscribed reader, much discussed in the reviews: young, female, aspiring to womanliness, ignorant, innocent of the physiological facts about sex, as well as being genteel, pious and intellectually unrobust. The required narrator was expected to collude with an implied (?parental) and hypocritical reader over this person's head so as 'not to bring a blush to her cheek', a much used criterion. With this inscribed reader in mind it was necessary to avoid even covert reference to parts of the female body other than the head or arms, to physiological facts such as menstruation, or to sexual relations even of a licit kind. The restrictive patterns of narrative syntax, to be dealt with in the next chapter, also relate to the preservation of the inscribed young person's ignorance not only of what is but of what goes on. This inscription of course was by no means perfect in practice.

But this common literary language is what 'speaks the man', in this case the male novelist who writes about women, already encoded in it. What I wish to show is that there occurs in some of Hardy's earlier novels (before *The Woodlanders*) a slippage which partly modifies signs and syntax. These half-changes create the fault-line perceived by feminist critics in his work. They create also contradictions which make available differing accounts of his treatment of women. In the rest of this chapter and Chapter 4 I shall deal with the slippage in relation to signs for femininity; in Chapter 3 as it relates to narrative syntax. The second half of the book will deal with the same topics in the later novels to show how the fault-line became an earthquake that shattered novelistic language.

Hardy's early novels, then, are characterised by an overt acceptance of current signs of 'woman' as idealised inferiors. But the ideal comes to him with a fresh gloss on it as the new, 'scientific', view. For there were those like Herbert Spencer, the populariser of Darwinian views (much read and copied out by Hardy), who with all the detachment of a committed sociologist 'justified' traditional misogyny scientifically. Not deterred by the demonstrated fruitlessness of discussion about comparative female/male brain-weights he explains in detail 'the comparative psychology of the sexes'. A few pages in his popular *The Study of Sociology* (first published 1873) set out to demonstrate that the view that 'men and women are mentally alike, is as untrue as that they are alike bodily' (Spencer, 1897, p.373). The differences are scientifically accounted for by two evolutionary 'facts': the woman's adaptation to her maternal role, and a more generalised adaptation, necessary for survival. In order to adapt women for motherhood, according to him, female evolution is cut short 'while there is yet a considerable margin of nutrition', otherwise there could be no offspring (*ibid.* p.374). So the brain is less and this results in less 'power of abstract reasoning' and less possession of 'the sentiment of justice – the sentiment which regulates conduct irrespective of personal attachments' (*ibid.* p.374). There is a mental specialisation in that women respond to infant helplessness, men to helplessness in general (*ibid.* pp.374–5).

The other psychological differences between the sexes are those which grow out of their relation as stronger and weaker in the evolutionary process. Men to survive had to be 'powerful . . . courageous . . . aggressive, unscrupulous, intensely egotistic'. In the struggle between them those men conquered 'in whom the brutal characteristics were dominant'. Women to survive had to learn as 'the wives of merciless savages' to disguise their feelings, to conceal their antagonisms, to be responsive quickly to others' feelings, to please and persuade (*ibid.* p.375). Since survival depended on the choice of the strongest brute, women developed a love of power in all its forms, a delight in submission and an extra capacity for awe. The latter had the useful effect of making them naturally more religious (*ibid.* pp.375–8). This somewhat ludicrous account is Spencer's 'justification' of his opening assertion.

And these 'mental characteristics', the reverse side of the womanly ideal, are on a superficial reading accepted by Hardy's early narrators. They provide a body of dogma from which explanations in the form of the infamous generalisations can be drawn. And the perceived need for explanations in *Desperate Remedies* (1871), *A Pair of Blue Eyes* (1873) and *Far from the Madding Crowd* (1874) is great; all negotiate a view of the nature of women which is assumed on one level to correspond to the womanly ideal and on another to be irrational, emotional and trivial. The balance sheet fluctuates: consequently these novels cannot be viewed chronologically but must be taken together as representative of a period in which, through shifting moods, Hardy struggles but fails to accept a patriarchal view. This is at its most extreme in the latest of the three novels in the (not unambivalent) treatment of Bathsheba (1874); it is at its most problematic in the story of Elfride (1873) which precedes this. The much noticed anti-women generalisations then disappear from the middle period novels: *The Trumpet Major* (1880), *A Laodicean* (1881), *Two on a Tower* (1882) and *The Mayor of Casterbridge* (1886), with which I shall not concern myself in this chapter. Eustacia Vye in *The Return of the Native* (1878) is a special case; and generalisations on women from *The Woodlanders* (1887) onwards will be shown later to be of a quite different kind from those in the early works.

These early explanations are often invoked where the text reveals a divergence of behaviour as between a woman and a man, or where a woman seems to act in a way that is superior, not inferior. When Cytherea and her brother are reduced to poverty by their father's death and he is forced to become a badly paid draughtsman and she a lady's maid, it is she who renounces bitterness: 'We can put up with being poor . . . if they only give us work to do . . . Yes, we desire as a blessing what was given us as a curse, and even that is denied. However, be cheerful.' (*Desperate Remedies*, p.79.) This resilience is dismissed, however, as a sign of inferiority because of a 'remembrance' of the essentialist view of woman as inferior:

> In justice to desponding men, it is as well to *remember* that the brighter endurance of women at these epochs – invaluable, sweet, angelic, as it is – owes more of its origin to a narrower vision that shuts out many of the leaden-eyed despairs in the van, than to a hopefulness intense enough to quell them. (*Desperate Remedies*, p.79, my emphasis.)

On the other hand, when Miss Aldclyffe acts ignobly in lying to Springrove about Cytherea's love for him, the general feminine interest in ends not in means is 'recognised' by the narrator:

> A fiery man in such a case would have relinquished persuasion and tried palpable force. A fiery woman added unscrupulousness and evolved daring strategy; and in her obstinacy, and to sustain herself as mistress, she descended to an action the meanness of which haunted her conscience to her dying hour. (*Ibid.* p.212.)

Coerced into a loveless but apparently appropriate marriage largely through love of her brother and in spite of her own feelings, Cytherea might seem set to win kudos as womanly when dressing prettily and carefully for the ceremony. On the contrary, reference to received doctrine draws out the significance of her action as an essential triviality. The narrator pontificates over this detail of behaviour and decides that this preoccupation with dress is one of the points

> in which a difference of sex amounts to a difference of nature . . . A man emasculated by coxcombry may spend more time upon the arrangement of his clothes than any woman, but even then there is no fetishism in his idea of them . . . But here was Cytherea . . . almost indifferent to life, yet possessing an instinct . . . to be particularly regardful of those sorry trifles, her robe, her flowers, her veil, and her gloves. (*Ibid.* pp. 250–1.)

Similarly Elfride's greater coolness in the face of her father's disapproval of Stephen is explained as only a meretricious superiority:

> Either from lack of the capacity to grasp the whole *coup d'oeil*, or from a natural endowment for certain kinds of stoicism, women are cooler than men in critical situations of the passive form. Probably,

in Elfride's case at least, it was blindness to the greater contingencies of the future she was preparing for herself. (*Ibid.* p.121.)

When torn between her two lovers her behaviour is ascribed not to a divided heart but something more well-known: 'Woman's ruling passion – to fascinate and influence those more powerful than she – though operant in Elfride, was decidedly purposeless.' (*Ibid.* p.202.)

Likewise, Bathsheba's dealings with Oak and Boldwood (whom she does not love) merely demonstrate a cardinal female characteristic: 'Women are never tired of bewailing man's fickleness in love, but they only seem to snub his constancy.' (*Far from the Madding Crowd*, p.182.) Her dealings with Troy (whom she does love) indicate, of course, female irrationality: 'Bathsheba, though she had too much understanding to be entirely governed by her womanliness, had too much womanliness to use her understanding to the best advantage.' (*Ibid.* p.207.) The two-sidedness of womanly intuitiveness shows through here in the use of *womanliness* not for intuitive understanding but for intuition seen as the pursuit of whim.

This conventional framework, however, does not dominate either *Desperate Remedies* or *A Pair of Blue Eyes*, or even *Far from the Madding Crowd*. The generalisations constitute one discourse among several and are set in a context that generates unease with the stereotype. The focus of this unease is the women themselves, haunted to pathos by the myth of complementarity expressed in the *North British Review*'s 'the more a man . . .' (1851, cited above), and inherent in Spencer's comparative account. A man needs woman's female nature to supplement his own; to subvert her role is to subvert his status and the structure they both inhabit; her womanliness defines his manliness as the negative always defines the positive; there is no space for deviation. And women in these three novels have a strong sense of contour to be conformed to in complementing the choosing male whom, in theory, they choose. The novelistic language has a gap for a certain feminine sign which will fill a place predetermined in detail by the lover: he specifies. So Cytherea anxiously asks her brother what Springrove's specifications for a wife are. She is told:

O, he says she must be girlish and artless: yet he would be loth to do without a dash of womanly subtlety . . . she must have womanly cleverness. 'And yet I should like her to blush if only a cock-sparrow were to look at her hard . . . a child among pleasures and a woman among pains was the rough outline of his requirement'. (*Desperate Remedies*, p.53.)

He has in mind also 'temper, hair, and eyes' (*ibid*. p.55) and the 'architectural designer's image' becomes 'very pervasive' (*ibid*. p.54) with the placeless girl. She is anxious to conform, not to be 'misconstrued' as the wrong sign and so lose her future place: 'She is timidly careful over what she says and does, lest she should be misconstrued or under-rated to the breadth of a shadow of a hair.' (*Ibid*. p.70.) Already the prevailing claims of the male to extract a perfect match for his image are undercut by the narrator's recognition of the anxiety they cause.

The irrationally exacting nature of the predetermined physical image is mocked in *A Pair of Blue Eyes*, where Elfride expects Knight to specify his preferred eye and hair colours. He is provided with a perfect weapon when she hazards the question and is told that he prefers dark hair to her own brown and hazel eyes to her own blue: 'Elfride was thoroughly vexed. She could not but be struck with the honesty of his opinions, and the worst of it was, that the more they went against her, the more she respected them.' (*Ibid*, p.190.) In recognising this the narrator recognises more than vanity, a deep sense of disvaluing: 'Elfride's mind had been impregnated with sentiments of her own smallness to an uncomfortable degree of distinctness, and her discomfort was visible in her face.' (*Ibid*. p.191.)

The pervasive presence of a system of particularised difference into which the individuals, Cytherea and Elfride, strain to squeeze themselves is present to the narrator as constraint not fulfilment. Even Bathsheba is haunted by it: this cool negotiator in the market place and fearless rider is alarmed by her maid's accurately Amazonian picture of her, and asks anxiously whether she is too bold and 'mannish' (*Far from the Madding Crowd*, p.217). For her as for the other women, the very qualities and characteristics which are defects in terms of the complementary system represent her own claim to a purely personal life. Bathsheba *is* to some extent Amazonian. In the same way

Elfride's authorship of a romance is her only autonomous life
and she feels it so. Yet since she discovers it to be superfluous
to what Knight requires in a woman she pesters herself 'with
endeavours to perceive more distinctly his conception of her as
a woman apart from an author: whether he really despised her;
whether he thought more or less of her than of ordinary young
women who never ventured into the fire of criticism at all' (*A
Pair of Blue Eyes*, p.166).

The same narratorial ambivalence is evident also in the main
area where male designs require impossibilities from women. As
sexual beings women are often in fiction assumed to know
themselves only through male desire. The dogma behind this is
made plain by the apparently assenting narrator of *Far from the
Madding Crowd* as a causal explanation of Bathsheba's behaviour
to one suitor:

> Boldwood as a means to marriage was unexceptional: she esteemed
> and liked him, yet she did not want him. It appears that ordinary
> men take wives because possession is not possible without marriage,
> and that ordinary women accept husbands because marriage is not
> possible without possession. (*Far from the Madding Crowd*, p.155.)

Yet the heroines of the three novels are palpitating in their
response to the men that attract them. This is made evident by
the narrators' sub-erotic description of them as tremblingly
beautiful, even pathetic, in their responsiveness. This admiration
destabilises statements like that last quoted, in which the narrator
attempts to resist the notion of feminine sexuality. The instability
is evident when Elfride fires 'a small Troy' in Smith's heart and
her own emotions are 'sudden as his in kindling'. Convoluted
explaining away is needed – she quickens but condemns herself:
'The least of women's lesser infirmities – love of admiration –
caused an inflammable disposition on his part, so exactly similar
to her own, to appear as meritorious in him as modesty made
her own seem culpable in her.' (*A Pair of Blue Eyes*, p.49.) A
similar confusion infects Cytherea's physical reaction to Springrove as she blushes 'a series of minute blushes' and shows 'the
usual signs of perplexity in a matter of the emotions' (*Desperate
Remedies*, p.70). The narrator here gives himself away: there is
nothing 'usual', according to prevailing generalisations in

emotional perplexity in a womanly woman; the phrase is a recognition of the unnaturalness of the repression expected of her.

The same recognition is present in the recording of the corollary to what Poovey, following Astell, calls the 'mediate relation' of women to sexual desire (Poovey, 1984, p.4): that men cannot accept or approve spontaneous sexual warmth. Observing this code the narrator of *A Pair of Blue Eyes* shows both Smith and Knight outdoing even Angel Clare in their negative demands: Smith prefers Elfride to be unkissed and Knight says: 'Freedom from that experience was your attraction.' (*A Pair of Blue Eyes*, p.293.) By which he means the experience of even a previous engagement. The result of this insistence is to turn Elfride into a haunted though guiltless woman. Her 'happiness was sadly mutilated' (*ibid*. p.288) by Mrs Jethway's threat to reveal to Knight the existence of an earlier admirer: 'The thought enclosed her as a tomb whenever it presented itself to her perturbed brain' (*ibid*. p.301).

This central requirement of complementarity, that women should in the novel (though not in all medical literature) be only the medium for the expression of male sexuality, was also the clearest expression of the real power relationship between the two. Spencer had an explicit norm for this. To be dominated, originally only necessary, is now gratifying:

> Clearly, therefore, it has happened . . . that, among women unlike in their tastes, those who were fascinated by power, bodily or mental, and who married men able to protect them and their children, were more likely to survive in posterity than women to whom weaker men were pleasing . . . To this admiration for power, caused thus inevitably, is ascribable the fact sometimes commented upon as strange, that women will continue attached to men who use them ill, but whose brutality goes along with power, more than they will continue attached to weaker men who use them well. (Spencer, 1897, p.377.)

Hardy's early narrators, since they are looking for this significance in women's behaviour, of course find it. Even on a trivial occasion when Springrove commands Cytherea to disregard public opinion, her taste for the whip is perceived in a mild form: 'For almost the first time in her life she felt the charming sensation . . . of being compelled into an opinion by a man she loved.' (*Desperate Remedies*, p.71.) Manston, full of evil and 'animal' passion recognises in his pursuit of her that 'perseverance, if only systematic, was irresistible by womankind' (*ibid*. p.233).

But the narrator, while recognising this public wisdom, is infected by an instability that springs from distaste for exploitation. This is partly because of its implications for the proposed exploiter, man. It is a lack of taste for this practice that in *A Pair of Blue Eyes* causes Stephen to lose Elfride and the narrator speaks with paradoxical bitterness:

> His very kindness in letting her return was his offence. Elfride had her sex's love of sheer force in a man, however ill-directed; and at that critical juncture in London Stephen's only chance of retaining the ascendancy over her that his face and not his parts had acquired for him, would have been by . . . dragging her by the wrist to the rails of some altar, and peremptorily marrying her . . . Decision, however suicidal, has more charm for a woman than the most unequivocal Fabian success. (*A Pair of Blue Eyes*, p.143.)

A fuller discussion of this viewpoint will follow in Chapter 4, but sympathy with the unoppressive man, pity for the victim and contempt for the man gratified by oppression reinforce the destabilising of the conventional view. Cytherea, though praised for kissing the rod with delight in obedience to the Sermon on the Mount (*Desperate Remedies*, p.224) when accepting Springrove's defection, arouses unexpected feelings when she agrees to marry Manston to help her sick brother. Her womanly motive is to do good to two men whose lives she thinks 'were far more important than hers'. At this point the narrator's perception of the conventional power-relationship shifts as he sees what it means to the individual woman. He is almost angry at her self-neglect:

> Directly Cytherea had persuaded herself that a kind of heroic self-abnegation had to do with the matter, she became much more content in the consideration of it. A wilful indifference to the future was what really prevailed in her, ill and worn out, as she was, by the perpetual harassments of her sad fortune, and she regarded this indifference, as gushing natures will do under such circumstances, as genuine resignation and devotedness. (*Ibid*. p.237.)

Thus, this polemical discourse in Hardy's novels differs from generalisations about women in those of Trollope because of its oscillations. Recurrently it has an uneasy, almost fevered, note, turning even to the doubtful support of fragile generalisations about men. The argument is dangerous and runs the risk of proposing them as at their best weak; at their worst bullying; easily influenced; and in other ways suitable only for the irrational, manipulative creatures they have to contend with and indeed prefer. This shadow looms disturbingly: if a woman takes her colour from the man she is walking with, then what of the reverse? Negative deforms positive in this language.

For in the course of these four novels, in spite of the male narrator's theology of woman, he allows another discourse to emerge which speaks of how a sensitive woman may experience social and individual pressure upon her. Through him not polemic, but her new perceptions, begin to speak. This starts even among the lurid events of *Desperate Remedies*. Cytherea immediately upon her entry into Miss Aldclyffe's comfortable house as lady's maid, when she has yet to meet her employer, leans out of the open window, a Blessed Damozel in appearance but not, ironically, in state:

> She was thinking that nothing seemed worth while; that it was possible she might die in a workhouse; and what did it matter? The petty, vulgar details of servitude that she had just passed through, her dependence upon the whims of a strange woman, the necessity of quenching all individuality of character in herself, and relinquishing her own peculiar tastes to help on the wheel of this alien establishment, made her sick and sad. (*Ibid.* p.92.)

And at the height of that other pressure after the wedding ceremony with Manston (despite her love for Springrove) she speaks unexpectedly to the brother for whom she has acted, who has spoken for society:

> Yes – my duty to society . . . But ah, Owen, it is difficult to adjust our outer and inner life with perfect honesty to all! Though it may be right to care more for the benefit of the many than for the indulgence of your own single self, when you consider that the many, and duty to them, only exist to you through your own existence, what can be said? What do our own acquaintances care about us? Not much. I think of mine. Mine will now (do they learn all the wicked frailty of my heart in this affair) look at me, smile

sickly, and condemn me. And perhaps, far in time to come, when I am dead and gone, some other's accent, or some other's song, or thought, like an old one of mine, will carry them back to what I used to say, and hurt their hearts a little that they blamed me so soon. And they will pause just for an instant, and give a sigh to me, and think, 'Poor girl!' believing they do great justice to my memory by this. But they will never, never realize that it was my single opportunity of existence, as well as of doing my duty, which they are regarding; they will not feel that what to them is but a thought, easily held in those two words of pity, 'Poor girl!' was a whole life to me; as full of hours, minutes, and peculiar minutes, of hopes and dreads, smiles, whisperings, tears, as theirs: that it was my world, what is to them their world, and they in that life of mine, however much I cared for them, only as the thought I seem to them to be. Nobody can enter into another's nature truly, that's what is so grievous. (*Ibid.* pp.253–4.)

This slippage of Cytherea's 'outer and inner life' is the beginning of the crack in her self-perception. Momentarily she sees herself as something beyond what the convention allows. She checks it with the thought of the 'wicked frailty' of her heart, but cannot so erase from the novel the alternative discourse to which, as I show, this passage belongs. Owen has no compelling answer with his trite 'Well, it cannot be helped.' How the discourse is furthered I will discuss below and in the next chapter. The same antithetical and jarring note is struck increasingly in *A Pair of Blue Eyes* by Knight's Elfride, who is also asserting a disjunction between her inner and outer life, between the reading that is made of her and what she feels herself to be. Elfride, after a struggle to conceal her guileless past, speaks, like Cytherea, from her own experience and applies a different standard from the womanly image she has, like the rest, accepted.

Am I such a – mere characterless toy – as to have no attrac – tion in me, apart from – freshness? Haven't I brains? You said – I was clever and ingenious in my thoughts, and – isn't that anything? Have I not some beauty? I think I have a little – and I know I have – yes, I do! You have praised my voice, and my manner, and my accomplishments. Yet all these together are so much rubbish because I – accidentally saw a man before you! (*A Pair of Blue Eyes*, p.317.)

Even in the apparently misogynistic clamour of *Far from the*

Madding Crowd the new discourse speaks and destabilises the Spencerian framework. One point at which this becomes clear is when Bathsheba is forced into a promise to consider Boldwood. As with Cytherea her individual emotional experience is allowed utterance:

> Bathsheba was in a very peculiar state of mind . . . It is hardly too much to say that she felt coerced by a force stronger than her own will, not only into the act of promising upon this singularly remote and vague matter, but into the emotion of fancying that she ought to promise. When the weeks intervening between the night of this conversation and Christmas day began perceptibly to diminish, her anxiety and perplexity increased. (*Far from the Madding Crowd*, p.358.)

Boldwood's coercion is as evident as Knight's, though the perceived gap between Bathsheba's inner and outer life is never long sustained.

This recurrent slippage between the place prepared for individual women in the system of signification and their own moments of autonomous inner life is also coded as a revelation of the limits of men's language. The latter is seen as the only one available to women for self-expression, but, as Poole pointed out in an article in 1981, is unfitted by its view of the world to be an adequate means of expressing their feelings and desires. A literal absorption of this alien speech by women is illustrated in *Far from the Madding Crowd* at a point where Boldwood appropriates Bathsheba even when she barely knows him:

> He spoke to her in low tones, and she instinctively modulated her own to the same pitch, and her voice ultimately even caught the inflection of his. She was far from having a wish to appear mysteriously connected with him; but woman at the impressionable age gravitates to the larger body not only in her choice of words . . . but even in her shades of tone and humour . . . (*Ibid.* p.171.)

This language reads the world (and so speaks) under masculine categories, a fact that Bathsheba herself articulates when Boldwood later offers her a verbal choice of states of mind: 'Do you like me, or do you respect me?' A choice and no choice, as in so many options for women, lies here. All feelings assumed possible are now on verbal offer but none fits and she falters:

'I don't know – at least, I cannot tell you. It is difficult for a woman to define her feelings in language which is chiefly made by men to express theirs.' (*Ibid*. p.356.) The valentine she sends is an illustration of the constraints of masculine readings: Bathsheba's feminine meaning is flippant, but Boldwood reads it literally as an injunction to marry her and refuses to be deflected either from taking it seriously himself or from insisting that she ought to do the same.

Elfride, like Bathsheba, recognises a gap between her inner life and the language she has to use, though she does not ascribe it to men's appropriation of words. When being courted by Knight she says unexpectedly, 'Well, you know what I mean, even though my words are badly selected and commonplace . . . Because I utter commonplace words, you must not suppose I think only commonplace thoughts.' (*A Pair of Blue Eyes*, p.196.) But the ultimate entrapment for women in men's control of language is their assumption that from a woman 'no' can mean 'yes', if one prefers it. Conformity to male reality is thus ensured. Naturally Ethelberta, like the narrators, sees all this clearly and passes it on to Picotee:

> 'But I thought honesty was the best policy?' said Picotee.
> 'So it is, for the man's purpose. But don't you go believing in sayings, Picotee: they are all made by men, for their own advantages. Women who use public proverbs as a guide through events are those who have not ingenuity enough to make private ones as each event occurs.' (*The Hand of Ethelberta*, p.153.)

This cool demolition of the public proverbs about women over which Hardy's early narrators alternatively apologise or grow enthusiastic marks the end of their lavish use.

The intermittent expressions of woman's own 'uncomplementary' experience, at odds with the language of men, creates a discourse contradictory to that of the anti-feminine generalisations. This second and disturbing voice is given covert but powerful articulation in the early plots. Where the generalisations of men's words entrap, plots can sometimes release.

Aside from this central image two other feminine signs remain to be mentioned, which later became significant in Hardy's novels: the seductress and the fallen woman. The former,

Eustacia in *The Return of the Native*, shows almost all the feminine qualities identified by Spencer: lack of a sense of justice, absence of sound intellect, inability to see beyond the 'concrete and proximate' of jewels, Budmouth, Paris. Extreme capriciousness and love of admiration whether from the boy, her grandfather or Wildeve are constant characteristics. Where she deviates from the complementary ideal is in feeling passion spontaneously not vicariously. Strikingly this passion is not directed towards an individual: 'To be loved to madness – such was her great desire . . . And she seemed to long for the abstraction called passionate love more than for any particular lover.' (*The Return of the Native*, p.92.) She has of course given herself physically to Wildeve and threatens to withhold the gift: 'I won't give myself to you any more.' (*Ibid*. p.87.) But adrift, as the conventional narrator sees it, she has no sense of filling the place of complaisant mistress for him. The other place that she might fill – as Clym's wife – is one which in an unwomanly way she tries to reshape. Yet she carries none of the meaning of the fallen woman. For such connotations the narrator substitutes a welter of pagan mythological imagery which erases it. If she is not the Angel, he asserts, she is the Goddess.

This evasion parallels that which takes place in the account of Fanny Robin whom Troy has seduced in *Far from the Madding Crowd*. The traditional significance of such figures – guilt, self-hatred, remorse, self-destructiveness – is replaced by the emblematic Fanny whose play as a sign is limited to pictures and surfaces: her sad and fruitless visits to the barrack and the church, her painful journey to the poorhouse where she dies. She lives in the feminine climate of anxiety in her desire to marry Troy, but her self-perception is never revealed. Thus, with the two signs which might negatively identify the womanly positive, Hardy refuses to draw on the conventional code.

CHAPTER THREE

Narrative Syntax in the Early Novels

The signification of women, described in Chapter 2, does not exist in the novelistic language system merely as an inventory: it is part of a grouping into larger units comparable to the building of phrasal categories into sentences. For these narrative structures patterns were already in stock, the most recurrent being that in which a woman chooses from amongst spurious multiple options. Since these all take male form, each option is the same option – a master/husband. Trollope's narrator in *The Vicar of Bullhampton* (1870) captures the collapse of choice when he envisages a girl asking 'what shall she do with her life?' The proposed answer shows that it is not the world that is her oyster but marriage that is her world. It is 'so natural' that she should reply to herself by saying 'that she will get married and give her life to somebody else . . . Nature prompts the desire, the world acknowledges its ubiquity, circumstances show that it is reasonable, the whole theory of creation requires it' (*The Vicar of Bullhampton*, 1924, pp. 259–60). Similarly, the choice is not a free choice since the men choose first. With the less frequent sequences where an unwomanly or fallen woman atones, the active form is again misleading, since her status is that of an object, the recipient of her punishment, whether it be death or some equivalent.

Critics who see Hardy as punishing women by his plots seem to have in mind these two normative patterns though they do not describe them as I have done. Typical criticism levelled against the first type is that directed by Wittenberg at *Desperate*

26

Remedies, a choice from among multiple suitors. Her grounds are that though early on Cytherea shows a spirited desire to preserve some measure of psychic independence, she is subjected to 'narrative manipulations' (Wittenberg, 1982, p.53) and leaves others to control her fate in ways 'not fully consonant with her character as originally presented' (*ibid*. p.54). This *ad hoc* argument misses a more radical objection that can be made to the pattern itself under certain conditions and misses the particular role of plot in Hardy's first published novel. I regard the interpretation as an over-simplification, resulting from a failure to consider the nature of plot and its place in the set of narrative discourses that constitutes a novel. I also believe that in Hardy's work plot becomes a coding of much that was not explicitly articulated. It captures on its own level some of the ambivalences already described, and pushes them to extremes more daring than the commentary. I shall, therefore, return to Wittenberg's specific account of Cytherea after some more general discussion. The implications of her criticism are that the narrator is to be equated with Hardy, and that plot is both narrator-generated and volitional on his part – what he wants to happen does. The second and third of these assumptions invite the consideration that the first long ago received, and which resulted in the general recognition that the narrator (reliable or unreliable) lies on this side of interpretation, separate from even an implied author.

This means that a narrative text always implies that the narrator is subordinate to the set of events, the 'nontextual given' that he is recounting, to use Culler's term (Culler, 1981, p.171), or the *fabula*, *histoire*, *story stuff*. There is potentially a struggle between all narrators and the events they tell of, a struggle usually to appropriate them under the narrator's own description. An illustration of a narrator who succeeds in effortless appropriation is found in Austen's *Persuasion* (1818) where nothing exists in the text that is not processed through her authoritative female consciousness. Similarly Trollope's narrator in *Ayala's Angel* appropriates relations between men and women under a Ruskinian explanation of women. Hardy's early narrators adopt, characteristically, a position of weakness from which to start. At the opening of *Desperate Remedies* the reader is immediately assumed to be in need of reassurance: 'In the long and intricately inwrought chain of circumstance which renders worthy of record some experiences of Cytherea Graye, Edward Springrove and others, the first event directly influencing the issue was a Christmas visit.' (*Desperate Remedies*, p.37.) This assertion claims priority for the visit over other possible beginnings but in doing so suggests some intractability in events: they might be seen by another as beginning at some other, more significant, point. The narrator of *A Pair of Blue Eyes* also feels a need to justify the stage at which he chooses to embark on his account of events: 'The point in Elfride Swancourt's life at which a deeper current may be said to have permanently set in, was one winter afternoon when she found herself standing . . . face to face with a man she had never seen before.' (*A Pair of Blue Eyes*, p.36.) The obvious contrivance here draws attention to the struggle to exert control which continues in the narrator's sustained but unsuccessful efforts to explain what goes on by a Spencerian account of women. Success is only partial because sympathy with women whose perceptions and volitions become, in Spencer's terms, deviant, overrides the generalisations.

In considering plot it is a mistake to focus initially on specific events considered in isolation – Cytherea's later passivity, Tess's death. What is more important is to relate them to underlying structures. When Hardy began to write women-centred novels in the 1860s, he did not start with infinite numbers of patterns of narrative syntax, any more than a speaker starts with infinite syntactic structures, though she may produce infinite numbers of sentences. The two patterns described above were part of a repertoire available in the nineteenth century, and Hardy in his early dealings with publishers is a novice trying to acquire control of it. Plot looms large even through absence: *The Poor Man and the Lady* was originally subtitled 'A Story with No Plot'.

Out of the repertoire Hardy in early novels chose most frequently the two examples of narrative syntax already described. Most often he uses the commonest type in which a woman selects a husband from two or more suitors: in *Desperate Remedies, Under the Greenwood Tree, A Pair of Blue Eyes, Far from the Madding Crowd, The Hand of Ethelberta, The Trumpet Major, A Laodicean*. The other frequent type in which a fallen woman pays the price is found in *Far from the Madding Crowd*, *The Return of the Native*, *The Mayor of Casterbridge*, *A Pair of Blue Eyes* and *Two on a Tower*. My approach will be to examine these in relation to the underlying structures of which they are exponents, and in which a linguistic deception is involved by a surface presentation of women as agents. I believe that in these novels the deep structure is either qualified or radically transformed by Hardy. I propose to discuss each pattern and its output in turn. I hope to show that the first pattern, as expounded in the early novels discussed in Chapter 2, enhances in varying degrees the subversive discourse identified there. The second pattern is similarly subjected to qualification and transformation in some of those novels as well as in *The Mayor of Casterbridge* and *Two on a Tower*.

The least problematic version in Hardy's work of the choice-of-a-husband story is *Under the Greenwood Tree*, in which Fancy Day oscillates between three self-selected suitors. The nearest to her in age and class, Dick Dewy, is distinguished by 'an ordinary-shaped nose, an ordinary chin, an ordinary neck, and ordinary shoulders' (*Under the Greenwood Tree*, p.33). His ordinariness is a test for Fancy who, the text directs, must in a womanly way overcome her dislike of it and her (venal) aspirations to something more glamorous. Dick's known rival is Frederic Shiner, older and, by implication, 'unsuitable': 'age about thirty-five, farmer and churchwarden, a character principally composed of a crimson stare, vigorous breath . . . with a mouth hanging on a dark smile but never smiling' (*ibid*. pp. 66–7). His undesirableness is a function of Fancy's feminine wilfulness in using him to make Dick jealous. The latter's unknown rival is the vicar, Maybold, who represents, like Fitzpiers, the lure of a higher social class. He has a certain inbuilt unsuitability: 'a good-looking young man with courageous eyes, timid mouth, and neutral nose' (*ibid*. p.93). Naturally he is too good for Fancy but serves to illustrate her capriciousness in engaging herself to him as well as to Dewy. An apparent peripety occurs when the latter is reduced to such misery that his brain is almost 'clarified' so that he nearly becomes once more 'a free man' (*ibid*. p.145). He asserts himself, and Fancy gives up her enjoyable game of tormenting him in a speech demonstrative of the charm of feminine irrationality:

> O Dick, directly you were gone I thought I had offended you and
> I put down the dress . . . and I ran after you . . . but I was too
> far behind. O, I did wish the horrid bushes had been cut down so
> that I could see your dear shape again! . . . Then I kept wandering
> and wandering about, and it was dreadful misery. (*Ibid.* p.146).

This first taming has to be duplicated when, as Dewy's fiancée, she accepts Maybold's proposal. In her subsequent recantation she makes the misogynistic generalisation for the narrator by placing herself squarely among 'all women', whose nature (venally) leads them 'to love refinement of mind and manners' and 'elegant and pleasing' surroundings (*ibid.* p.176). As in the event Maybold withdraws, no appearance of choice is left anyway.

The implications of this narrative pattern when 'assertively' handled are now clear: that a husband is a woman's only goal and reward; that she must earn him in a peripety representing a return to the womanly ideal, and that (optionally) the husband should be of her own social class. The latter option is one often taken by Trollope but fraught with difficulty for Hardy. All these implications represent current ideologies, but plainly the text can only be read as reinforcing them if, as Belsey following Benveniste says, it is 'declarative' not 'interrogative' (Belsey, 1980, pp. 90–1). This requires two specific trajectories through events: the narrator's collusive impulse with what happens, and the women's subordinate desire following the same male-oriented course. In *Under the Greenwood Tree* Fancy's deepest wishes follow the line of events that lead to the right husband; her dealings with Shiner and, more especially, Maybold, are wrong but transient desires, not something she truly sanctions. This submits to the narrator's reading of events as examples of feminine capriciousness duly abandoned in a process of maturation. Potentially and as embodied in this novel the common narrative structure is, to a feminist, deeply tainted. It is also punitive in the specific sense that the preferred peripeties (like Fancy's) are those that show reproach, shame, disaster or pregnancy bringing a woman nicely to heel.

Traces of a modification of this kind of assertive treatment of the pattern are already seen in *Far from the Madding Crowd*, though this is often read as an ampler version of *Under the Greenwood Tree*, reinforcing even more emphatically the tainted implications outlined above. A summary of such readings prefaces one male critic's attempt to present 'A New View of Bathsheba Everdene' (Casagrande in Kramer, 1979): 'It has become commonplace among critics of Thomas Hardy's *Far from the Madding Crowd* . . . to say that Bathsheba Everdene, the novel's heroine, develops through misfortune and suffering from a vain, egotistical girl into a wise, sympathetic woman.' (Kramer, p.50.) The attachment of these 'redemptive' views to Bathsheba's amorous affairs provides intense reinforcement for the womanly ideal. But it is within the limits laid down by the critics referred to that Casagrande's 'new' view is placed. He manages to produce an even more reactionary reading than the old ones: woman (Bathsheba) is irredeemable, while Oak, the man she marries, manages to be duped by her and yet at the same time to be 'an example of how to cope with the imperfection of things':

> Is Hardy suggesting that Oak is but another triumph for 'a fair product of Nature in the feminine kind'? The answer must be yes, in part. The old vanity, seeking the self's re-embodiment in others, rather than in a mirror, still governs Bathsheba. But it must be seen that Oak, knowing this from the start, is a willing victim who enjoys his own kind of victory. If Bathsheba has not changed essentially through some three years of severe schooling, her circumstances have changed significantly. Her circle of admirers has been reduced by two-thirds, and her 'absolute hunger' for affection, a genuine aspect of her flawed nature, can be satisfied only by Oak, the sole survivor of the original circle of worshippers. Oak has Bathsheba, so to speak, where he wants her – in a position in which she must turn to him for gratification of her infirm nature's deepest longing. (*Ibid*. pp. 69–70.)

This reading (including the final paradoxical reference to Oak as sexual blackmailer) is assigned to Hardy, but it is more punitive by far than the text. The latter is not free of qualification at moments when the victimisation of Bathsheba is made evident and on the occasions when she rejects men's words for her experience.

Casagrande's account also ignores the questioning of causality that is spelt out in the novel. The narrator comments on Boldwood's reaction to the valentine:

Material causes and emotional effects are not to be arranged in regular equation. The result from capital employed in the production of any movement of a mental nature is sometimes as tremendous as the cause itself is absurdly minute. When women are in a freakish mood their usual intuition, either from carelessness or inherent defect, seemingly fails to teach them this, and hence it was that Bathsheba was fated to be astonished to-day. (*Far from the Madding Crowd*, p.143.)

The rebuke in the tail of this does not invalidate the generalisation, which counters any interpretation that sees the events of the novel – storm, fire, an unfaithful husband, emotional blackmail, widowhood – as a neatly organised series of circumstantial knocks designed to bring Bathsheba into a state of sobriety and submission. The passage makes explicit a characteristically Hardyan feature of plot viewed as a possibly causal sequence of events: the sense of disproportion between action and 'consequences' that makes questions about responsibility unanswerable. Bathsheba, like others involved in precipitating lurid happenings, is herself a victim of this disjunction. Thus conventional, punitive readings of this novel are only sustained by ignoring important contradictory elements that question them.

Even less easy to sustain is a reading of *Desperate Remedies* as a text that reinforces patriarchy. In fact it is already on a superficial level a mixture of two narrative patterns: the one so far discussed and the enigma-solving sensation type. The former appears as the sequence of events relating to Cytherea Graye as wife material; the latter as a sequence (including most of the same events) unravelling the murderous and bigamous activities of Aeneas Manston, illegitimate son of Miss Aldclyffe, Cytherea's employer. Plots as strings of events preoccupied Hardy and showing his usual timidity in interpreting his own novels, he speaks in the *Early Life* of having taken too literally Meredith's advice to write a novel with 'more plot' than *The Poor Man and the Lady* and constructing the 'eminently "sensational" plot' of this work (*Early Life*, 1928, p.83). He focuses moreover on the junction of the two plots as the cause of hostile criticism by *The Spectator*: 'the reason for this violence being mainly the author's daring to suppose it possible that an unmarried lady owning an estate could have an illegitimate child' (*ibid.* p.110). Such a focus is true to the text: Cytherea Aldclyffe effects the junction of the two patterns, forming a node from which both spring. Their interrelation modifies startlingly the multiple-suitor pattern for which Hardy chooses three exponents: Edward Springrove, the architect's assistant, whom Cytherea prefers but who is passively engaged to a richer girl; his passionate rival, Manston, a bigamist murderer; and Manston's mother, Miss Aldclyffe. She, before her illegitimate son arrives, invites Cytherea to her bed in the least covertly sexual scene in the early novels. Like many well known Victorian males she has a preference for virgins and is horrified to find that the girl has been in love already:

> Yes, women are all alike. I thought I had at last found an artless woman who had not been sullied by a man's lips, and who had not practised or been practised upon by the arts which ruin all the truth and sweetness and goodness in us . . . O Cytherea, can it be that you, too, are like the rest? (*Desperate Remedies*, p.109.)

This strange trio of would-be lovers figures sharply the monstrous nature of the pseudo-choices offered to heroines by the assertive form of the commonest narrative sentence.

The specific feminist objection made by Wittenberg to the events in the later part (which show Cytherea as passive and submissive) deals only partially with the question of her volitions, of what throughout she wishes her story to be. The novel, however, shows precisely her fluctuating impulse, evoking an early stage on the way to autonomy: a temporary overcoming of guilt about her deep desire on the eve of her marriage for an unwomanly freedom to choose. The sequence of self-assertion at a time of crisis followed by guilty retraction captures a precarious moment and anticipates in little the assertion and retraction of Sue Bridehead. Hardy catches this phase as Cytherea speaks to her brother about marrying Manston and then also the collapse under pressure as she reverts guiltily to 'doing her best'. Her volitions fail and fade and the choices are made by others.

After Manston's death Cytherea is free to marry the spiritless and not entirely faithful Springrove; the chattel she has become is duly handed over to him. This is a marriage that the conventional narrator would underwrite as Cytherea's reward for her return to womanliness. In contrast to the end of *Far from the Madding Crowd*, this part of the text seems to be a narratorless sentence. The final chapter is in two sections: a description of the wedding by the local bell-ringers and a piece of unsupported dialogue between Cytherea and Springrove, superimposing an earlier pre-betrayal picture on the sullied present: 'Ah, darling, I remember exactly how I kissed you that first time . . . You were there as you are now . . . Then I put my cheek against that cheek, and turned my two lips round upon those two lips, and kissed them – so.' (*Ibid.* pp.389–90.) The conventional implications of such a plot, described earlier, meet with no collusion at this crucial stage. Exaggeratedly trite pictures replace them, as well as dialogues with which the narrator refuses to collude. The disturbing specificity of the murder plot enhances the openness of this ending: logically the mystery is solved but its precise horrors make an intrusive background to the wedding photograph.

The total transformation of the most familiar narrative sentence occurs in *The Hand of Ethelberta*. Hardy's 'Comedy in Chapters' turns pseudo-active into real active and so undermines the assertiveness of the text. The linguistic change is mirrored in the ambiguous title: the surface pattern points to the old pseudo-passive meaning, with Ethelberta's hand given passively in marriage; whereas the implications of the text point to the real active force, as the hand seizes everything within its grasp. Like Cytherea, Bathsheba and Elfride before her, she chooses a husband but, as I hope to show, her choice is a real one. Further, the narrative offers new trajectories through events, originating in the heroine not the narrator, unlike those of earlier novels. The usual implications of the pattern are subverted.

On the surface things look conventional: Ethelberta has four suitors; Christopher Julian, an impoverished but educated and sensitive musician, Neigh and Ladywell, two society men, and Lord Mountclere, rich, old and dissolute. The built-in expectation of the structure is that Julian will be the right husband. On the surface too Ethelberta's suitors are as usual self-selected and this seems, in fact, to be true of the long-standing affection that Julian feels. But, in reality, with the other three agency is in the woman's hands as she draws them into her orbit by a particular kind of unconventional behaviour and mimes emotional and physical availability. She is enabled to do this by a degree of independence which would not normally be hers socially since she is a member of a family of manual labourers and domestic servants, by being the widow of a man of rank in whose family she was a governess. Her marriage has given her social though not financial freedom. It is her enhanced status that makes it possible for her to behave in what is perceived as an outrageously self-publicising way: to hire herself out as a story-teller before the public. Her appearances in this guise evoke a mixture of disapproval and titillation at a perceived illicit exposure. She is treated as 'a new sensation' like 'the latest conjurer, spirit-medium, aëronaut, giant, dwarf, or monarch' (*The Hand of Ethelberta*, p.130), a kind of pit-girl in trousers. A woman story-teller is described by a fictional reviewer in this spirit: 'A handsome woman . . . may have her own reasons for causing the flesh of the London public to creep upon its bones by her undoubtedly remarkable narrative powers; but we question if much good can result from such a form of entertainment.' (*Ibid.* p.130.)

In some sense Ethelberta is determined to sell herself and in this episode there is a strong suggestion from other women that she exhibits herself like a prostitute. Julian's sister is one of these critics:

Faith, who had secret doubts about the absolute necessity of Ethelberta's appearance in public, said, with remote meanings, 'Perhaps it is not altogether a severe punishment to her to be looked at by well-dressed men. Suppose she feels it as a blessing, instead of an affliction?' (*Ibid.* p.129.)

Ethelberta's mother also speaks in terms appropriate to a sexual fall when she expresses a fear that the story-telling activities, if combined with the revelation that she is not a lady, will take away the family's good name as 'simple country folk' and interfere with her sisters' chances in domestic service. Yet it is the unwomanly act of making herself available that, by enhancing the perception of her as anomalous, captures the attentions of Neigh, Ladywell and Mountclere. And since all three are initially gulled by her deception about identity, their courtship appears to be primarily the result of her manipulations. She has truly taken over the role of agent in drawing them on.

The usual peripety (where the heroine undergoes a chastening, leading to conformity and the right husband) is also transformed. Its ghost is there, since Ethelberta suffers an epiphany resulting in marriage. But this general form of the pattern has here exponents that confound patriarchal values. The narrative sequence hinges on the choice of a husband in which the suppression of part of Ethelberta takes place. But what is overcome is, placing aside family affections, her deepest feeling. It is clear from early on that she loves Christopher Julian, of whom she first confesses to her sister, Picotee, that she hates him less than any other man, and later that he is the only man 'whose wife I should care to be' (ibid. p.161). There is a continued sub-text in the novel evoking the difficulties and pleasures of their relationship, which the choice of a husband ends. Whereas she shows a ruthless practicality about her dead husband – 'Ought I not to show a little new life when my husband died in the honeymoon?' (ibid. p.98) – she is tempted to be capriciously 'womanly' with Julian. However, she stops playing this role when Mountclere 'earnestly' asks her to marry him. With the unwomanly coolness she has shown only to others she now weighs Julian against Mountclere:

> There lay open to her two directions in which to move. She might annex herself to the easy-going high by wedding an old nobleman, or she might join for good and all the easy-going low, by plunging back to the level of her family, giving up all her ambitions for them, settling as the wife of a provincial music-master named Julian, with a little shop of fiddles and flutes . . . And each of these divergent grooves had its fascinations, till she reflected with regard to the first that, even though she were a legal and indisputable Lady Mountclere, she might be despised by my lord's circle, and left lone and lorn. (Ibid. pp.279–80.)

She struggles long and painfully to decide between the two as Cytherea did against her love for Springrove, 'rightly' indulged in the end; and as Bathsheba did against her love for Troy, 'wrongly' indulged and therefore punished in the end. For Ethelberta the instrument of final resolution is not a surge of passionate feeling, though Christopher is presented as a worthy object of love and her feelings as strong. Mountclere is unlikely to bring personal happiness but very likely to produce financial benefit to her family; she needs a criterion to apply in order to make a choice between the alternatives represented by saying yes or no to him. With impeccable logic she turns at this point to philosophy, specifically to J. S. Mill on *Utilitarianism* (1861), discovering there the idea that morality lies in the application of a standard of disinterested benevolence which the agent considers in order to act for the happiness of all concerned, not simply herself. This leads her to conclude that since more people will benefit from her marrying than her not marrying Mountclere, her union with him is expedient. This crucial decision as to the placing of her hand in marriage is therefore a triumph of logic over love, 'masculine' reason over the softer womanly virtues. Ethelberta is not a woman whose errant impulses are suppressed for the sake of conformity with the events that are to befall her. That would be so if she had decided to marry the man she loves. On the contrary she is a woman to whose will events are seen largely to conform. That is how Picotee sees her finally, as 'an eternal Providence' (*The Hand of Ethelberta*, p.393).

A minor impediment appears in her projected course when after the marriage with Mountclere she discovers, as she thinks, a resident mistress and attempts to renege by running away. She quickly resolves this when Mountclere outwits her and further explains that the other woman is banished. She accepts the compromise which is already a corollary of her decision to marry him in the first place: 'That sounds well. Lord Mountclere, we may as well compromise matters' (*ibid*. p.383). The flawed outcome, which she had anticipated, gives her precisely what she intended: security for her family, status, money and control of her husband for herself, in place of emotional fulfilment.

Her comet-like determination sweeps through the novel's last stages, reversing the usual hierarchy of voices between narrators and heroines. The narrator's early volitions seem, like those of her suitors, to be largely dictated by hers and he finally loses control of events: it passes to her after his disparaging comment on the 'misapplication of sound and wide reasoning' in the crucial decision (*ibid*. p.285). There is no attempt to account for what goes on by misogynistic generalisations. The narrating voice is virtually absent from the end of the novel, leaving the same openness as in *Desperate Remedies*. Like most other males in the novel the narrator appears to be appropriated by the omnicompetent Ethelberta. So, she chooses a husband; she seizes him rather than earns him; and she fixes on one whose age, class and character make him entirely unsuitable in conventional terms. The ludic embodiment in events of these implications boldly asserts the negative of all that the pattern usually implies and the values that it usually enforces.

The much less common type of narrative is that in which a woman who has proved morally defective in a specifically sexual way acts by repenting or atoning through shame, guilt, self-hatred, good works or forms of self-immolation and/or death or exile. Under one view this is linguistically a sub-class of the type of narrative already discussed, since it too is a pseudo-active with the woman only superficially in an agent/subject role and since, as Penny Boumelha sees it, marriage and death are interchangeable as endings. The fictional sentence here providing the narrative string was spelt out by W. H. Mallock late in the period in the second sentence of the following passage:

> In the English fiction of today it is a universal rule that the men, and especially the women, with whom the reader is intended to sympathize, shall all stop short of one another at a certain point, whatever may be their dispositions . . . It is also a rule equally universal that any grave transgression of the moral code shall entail on its transgressors some appropriate punishment. (Frierson in Owens, 1968, p.47.)

Several of Hardy's earlier novels have this as their main narrative structure or as embeddings within it. Only in *A Pair of Blue Eyes* and *Two on a Tower* is the matrix of the narrative the premature death of a female figure whose dealings with men have been perceived as blameworthy. Fanny, Eustacia and Lucetta require, however, similar consideration in minor structures. Normative examples of the pattern are the stories of Dickens' Emily and Martha in *David Copperfield* (1850), Alice Marwood in *Dombey and Son* (1848), Gaskell's Esther in *Mary Barton* (1848). Such instances reveal, as *Under the Greenwood Tree* did with the earlier pattern, what the implications of an assertive text like these are: that women are up for moral assessment; that their sexual behaviour is the determining factor; that when they prove defective in this respect they are rightly destroyed from within by shame and guilt and eradicated from without by exile, death, disappearance. Already by the mid-nineteenth century interrogative exponents of this narrative sentence existed, in such works as Gaskell's *Ruth* (1853) or Eliot's *The Mill on the Floss* (1860), as well as in some less serious sensation novels. But the continued dominance of the assertive force is evidenced by critics hostile to it, yet driven to attack it as the literary status quo:

> . . . provided a woman, however young, however ignorant in the world's ways . . . has unloosed for one moment the girdle of her maiden innocence, – though the lapse may have been instantaneous, delirious, instantly repented and resolutely retrieved . . . she is punished without discrimination as the most sunk of all sinners; and . . . all writers of fiction represent her as acquiescing in the justice of the sentence. (Helsinger, 1983, vol.3, p.120.)

What I hope to show is that the process of change in the illocutionary force of plots of this type, their real communicative purpose, is furthered by Hardy, a fact not generally recognised; though feminist critics of George Eliot, for instance, produce a sophisticated range of readings of the connection between sexual fault and death in her novels. These are summarised in Maggie Tulliver's case by Boumelha: 'a revenge murder of Tom; a narrator's murder of Maggie, the destruction of the restrictive community, the fulfilment of an incest fantasy; regression to a pre-pubertal age without sexual difference . . .' (Roe, 1987, p.29). But with Hardy the punitive interpretation (sometimes modified) holds sway among critics. This is perverse, given Hardy's obsession with the difficulty of understanding the relationship between events in a linear sequence; he reverts repeatedly in the *Early Life* to the idea that since nothing 'bears out in practice what it promises incipiently' he is 'content with tentativeness from day to day' (*Early Life*, p.201). Even in conventional novels the deaths of fallen women are often a source of unease: Auerbach (1980) for instance reads some of them as romantic examples of the 'figurehead of a fallen culture', a coding that contradicts the flexible reality of history in which such women might become respectable wives (Auerbach, 1980, p.31). Such romanticising is evident in minor figures in Hardy's work. Fanny Robin has already undergone a complete sexual fall before she appears, so that the problem of the sexual encounter and its associations, so fatal to *Ruth*, never arises. Sheared of inner life, increasingly pictorial, garlanded with flowers, moving even the feelings of a dog, she qualifies literally by appearance for her mythic role. The serial editor's succinct decision to 'omit the baby' (Millgate, 1982, p.160) merely completes the asexual pathos which comprises the narrator's perception. Given this symbolism it is clear that responsibility for her death lies with Troy, blackened as the villain of the piece. It appears as the cruel destruction of an innocent, not well-justified punishment, and its consequences for Bathsheba and Troy bear this out.

Eustacia's death is another variant of the romanticising of the fallen woman. Her pictorial qualities as 'The Figure against the Sky' and 'Queen of Night' are iconographically equated with many goddesses. This 'model goddess', too, has already undergone a complete sexual fall offstage. Unlike Fanny she is all volition and (like Ethelberta) acts for part of the novel as a Providence goddess manipulating events, exerting control over the boy, Wildeve, Clym and, malignly, his mother. But all the options she creates are finally perceived by her as unsatisfactory. Her limitless and unfocused desire cannot be satisfied, as her attempt to elope with Wildeve reveals to her: 'Can I go, can I go? . . . He's not *great* enough for me to give myself to – he does not suffice for my desire! . . . If he had been a Saul or a Bonaparte – ah! But to break my marriage vow for him – it is too poor a luxury!' (*The Return of the Native*, p.357) The self-hatred of fallen women like Martha and Emily in *David Copperfield*, Esther in *Mary Barton*, moves on to something only superficially resembling it: 'How I have tried and tried to be a splendid woman, and how destiny has been against me! . . . I do not deserve my lot! . . . I was capable of much; but I have been injured and blighted and crushed by things beyond my control!' (*Ibid.* p.357.) Suicide becomes the larger, the self-created, the preferred option. In the description of her drowned body the narrator accepts her impressiveness as appropriate and artistically fitting on a visual level, and also as deeply symbolic: 'The stateliness of look which had been almost too marked for a dweller in a country domicile had at last found an artistically happy background.' (*Ibid*. pp.376–7.) Beside this view of her extinction as transfiguration, there are offered in the text also views of it as witchcraft and a flight from social pressure. These alternatives leave the novel open-ended and interrogative.

More ambiguous still is the sequence of events in *The Mayor of Casterbridge* that leads to Lucetta's death through a seizure caused by the skimmity ride which makes a public spectacle of her early relationship with Henchard. Her sexual fall predates her entry into the story, appearing now as indiscretion, now as something more. Her death involves her pregnancy by Farfrae, however, a fact quite unconnected with her fall and entirely legitimate. If the skimmity ride represents social retribution, that meaning is obscured by the identity of the perpetrators, inhabitants of Mixen Lane, powerfully evoked as the source of physical and moral poison in the town. Though her death is not picturesque like Fanny's, it is intensely pathetic, especially when it is made clear that the two men who loved her can easily put it behind them. Henchard's laconic reaction is to notice the irony of the fact that 'Death was to have the oyster, and Farfrae and himself the shells' (*The Mayor of Casterbridge*, p.291). Her beloved Farfrae is himself ironised for the prudentiality which takes him 'out of the dead blank' of his loss through the perception that 'by the death of Lucetta he had exchanged a looming misery for a simple sorrow' (*ibid*. p.304). Thus all sense of death as primarily well-deserved by the woman gives way to other more interrogative implications in these three texts.

In the two novels where the pattern under discussion is central, the tentative alterations in *Far from the Madding Crowd*, *The Return of the Native* and *The Mayor of Casterbridge* are replaced by more fundamental shifts in narrative syntax. Once more in them exponents of the pattern are modified to figure new implications. In *A Pair of Blue Eyes* Elfride's sexual defectiveness is in respect both of her reputation and her integrity. Her failed elopement with Stephen Smith will destroy her good name unless it is kept secret, though she has committed nothing but indiscretion. The affixing of a bad reputation in this arbitrary way is paralleled by the more radical condemnation under which Knight obsessively appropriates her moral being when he learns of her innocent dealings with Jethway and Smith. This ironising of the concept of sexual defectiveness is enhanced by the narrator's awareness of its faultiness. What he sees as her suffering is not guilt but anxiety, which hounds her to distraction when she follows Knight to London, wildly imagining her own power to reverse the double standard: 'O, could *I* but be the man and *you* the woman, I would not leave you for such a little fault as mine! . . . Ah, how I wish you could have run away with twenty women before you knew me, that I might show you I would think it no fault.' (*A Pair of Blue Eyes*, p.335.)

Sexual fall is followed by death on the usual pattern but an extra element is inserted which only comes to light after it has been revealed to the now repentant Smith and Knight: that before it Elfride has married a man who socially, financially and even physically outshines them. Smith, the workman's son, Knight, the man of letters, are superseded by Lord Luxellian who in the final scene of the novel turns them into figures of rejection as they approach her coffin.

> Beside the latter was the dark form of a man . . . his body flung across the coffin, his hands clasped, and his whole frame seemingly given up in utter abandonment to grief. He was still young – younger, perhaps, than Knight – and even now showed how graceful was his figure and symmetrical his build. (*Ibid*. p.373.)

The baldness and asymmetricality of Knight mentioned earlier spring to mind and his dispossession figures as a triumph for Elfride.

This is certainly how the narrator sees her marriage and death, with his constant playful insertion of the solemn black funeral van which so impedes Knight's and Smith's journey as they travel back to what they imagine is another chance to propose to Elfride. Instead they find themselves turned away from her coffin by the rich, handsome, loving, aristocratic husband she has acquired. They advance to where they had once stood beside Elfride on the day the three met. The place is the Luxellian vault, which is where Elfride belongs for more reasons than one. Triumph and escape are fused and agency is transferred back to her in death: 'She had herself gone down into silence like her ancestors, and shut her bright blue eyes for ever.' (*Ibid.* p.373.) The sequence of events in this novel mimes implications for the pattern totally opposite to that of *Ruth*. It is on one level a ludic resolution of the contradiction in the novel described in Chapter 2. Far from being punishing to women the narrative operates punitively against men.

Two on a Tower takes plot as figure a stage further. The basic components of the syntactic structure, fall and subsequent death are subject to an unusual transformation. It has been suggested that Lady Constantine's clandestine marriage to the aspiring astronomer, St Cleeve, so much younger and so far below her in social class, is a surrogate for an illicit love affair, with its urgent sexual attraction, secrecy, pregnancy. This ambiguity, however, is raised to a higher power by a series of sensational events which mean that their marriage is void because her absent first husband was not dead when they contracted it and that although she later knows this, she then yields 'to all the passion of her first union with him' (*Two on a Tower*, p.239) and becomes pregnant. This is only discovered when she has already sent St Cleeve away for a long period out of a disinterested desire to further his career. Like the rape–seduction in *Tess* this serves to question moral boundaries: the illicit and furtive legal embraces contrast with the spontaneous, unprudential passion of an act that circumstances of an unpredictable kind have rendered illicit. Viviette has appeared to become a fallen woman to the world as represented by her brother, Louis, who watches her clandestine meetings with St Cleeve; and has technically become so by circumstantial misfortune.

The fate of this doubly fallen woman who, in a deep sense is not fallen at all, is to marry a middle-aged bishop when too late she discovers her pregnancy. In doing this and attempting to pass off St Cleeve's child as the bishop's, she is striking at the safeguarding of legal paternity that underlies the sexual double standard. At Swithin's return, the discovery that in her thirties she is too old for him, merging into a momentary belief that his love is suddenly restored, kills her. This is the narrator's interpretation of events:

> Sympathize with her as he might, and as he unquestionably did, he loved her no longer. But why had she expected otherwise? 'O

woman,' might a prophet have said to her, 'great is thy faith if thou believest a junior lover's love will last five years!' (*Ibid*. p.274.)

The commentary dwells on the pathos of her 'worn and faded aspect' and how for Swithin this makes her 'not the original Viviette' (*ibid*. p.273). Hence the final words of the novel are an ironic interpretation (of what has been presented in terms of an emotional and personal betrayal) on a social level, where the sin against patrimony is the salient offence: 'Viviette was dead. The Bishop was avenged.' (*Ibid*. p.275.) An explicitly, perhaps ironically, punitive death is at issue here; but it is the man who inflicts it, not the narrator, and it is the cynically inscribed reader who regards it as appropriate revenge.

This contour is sharpened by a narratorial transposition of gender: Swithin young, helpless, naïve as well as sexually inexperienced is, in effect, seduced by the older, richer widow. It is she who takes all the initiatives, makes all the presents, cuts off a lock of his hair. In most respects she assumes the male role, but even given the external advantages usually belonging to a man, she cannot escape the biological consequences of being female: pregnancy and loss of sexual attractiveness. As in *A Pair of Blue Eyes* the complexity of the discourse provided by plot expresses on a different and disturbing level the doubts and ambivalences of a would-be Spencerian narrator. It is already evident that the significance of plot in Hardy's novels is more than a simple answer to, 'And what happened next?'

CHAPTER FOUR

Other Signs: the Poor Man and the Artist

Hardy's early novels, as I have shown, enact a contemporary confusion in the debate on the nature and duties of women. Relying on received wisdom they none the less develop a contradictory discourse which gives glimpses of the gap between 'ideal' and inner selves. In a few of the texts certain male figures are prominent as signs which have a meaning in Hardy's novelistic idiolect that is a variation on what is commonly found in the work of previous major novelists. Earlier, the poor man, like Stephen Blackpool in *Hard Times* (1854) or John Barton in *Mary Barton* (1848), is by default the sign for the whole working class (female as well as male) among whom he is placed and for whom he speaks. Hardy's poor man, as originally conceived, however, is simply an isolated and oppressed male who does not subsume the working-class woman into his signification. In the semantic field of social class the poor woman remains unaccounted for. Similarly his first portrait of a (literary) artist is one whose maleness is part of the meaning of the sign. But then the assumption of male identity through a *nom de plume* was still a familiar practice among women writers; invisibility here is not unexpected. It would have been unthinkable later in Hardy's life.

But as his early narratives proceed to describe the paradigm experience of these two male figures, it is seen to overlap with that of all women in some circumstances. This overlap causes a 'fuzziness' of meaning (such as that well-known between *cup* and *glass*) that often leads to semantic change. Gender boundaries

45

are broken down, with results that I shall describe. For this reason I regard the relations between these three terms as the ground for a transition between the early and late novels in their treatment of women. In this transition the narrator's role is vital, since it is he who attempts to manipulate the signs; in the event he undergoes an epiphany.

When earlier mainstream novelists confront some of the inequities of capitalist society they locate their narrators in a (compromising) position of unshakeable middle-class security. These speak as those undertaking 'a dangerous voyage of discovery into an uncharted working-class world' (Keating, 1971, p.33). Gaskell's narrator in *Mary Barton* does reach an uneasy awareness that her revelation of social ills undermines her own position. But, confusedly, she feels obliged to defend the factory owners (and by implication the middle-class) against the charge of their indifference to and responsibility for the sufferings of the working-class:

> I know that this is not really the case; and I know what is the truth in such matters: but what I wish to impress is what the workman feels and thinks. True, that with child-like improvidence, good times will often dissipate his grumbling, and make him forget all prudence and foresight. (Gaskell, *Mary Barton*, p.60.)

The location of Hardy's narrators when class is at issue is different even from this (which is already a variant on the conventional). Their viewpoint and perceptions relate to two social scales. One of these is Gaskell's (and others') which in spite of her fine moral discriminations distinguishes primarily her own 'us' from 'them', and includes a gap unbridgeable except momentarily on the level of personal emotion. But Hardy, born into a rural society, sees gradations within the working class itself. When in 1881 Charles Kegan Paul referred to him romantically (in the *British Quarterly Review*) as 'sprung of a race of labouring men' (Millgate, 1982, p.202) Hardy was stung to write and tell him at once that

> My father is one of the last of the old 'master-masons' left . . . From time immemorial . . . my direct ancestors have all been master-masons, with a set of journeymen masons under them: though they have never risen above this level, they have *never* sunk below it –

i.e. they have never been journeymen themselves. (*Letters*, vol.1, p.89.)

These 'castes' were important in his original personal scale, and he was still describing in 1927 how they had been distinguished in his youth: 'The two castes rarely inter-married and did not go to each other's house gatherings save exceptionally' (Millgate, 1982, p.26). A feature of this second scale as illustrated by Hardy's own experience was that it saw a gap but assumed it to be bridgeable by men of talent.

As a poor man of lower-class origin the conventional scale must have been brought home to Hardy at the latest in 1872 when he asked John Gifford, Emma's father and a solicitor, for permission to marry her. There is reliable evidence that Gifford later referred to his son-in-law as a 'low-born churl who has presumed to marry into *my* family' (*ibid*. p.143). As an artist, he must already have extrapolated the existence of this alternative view of society from the history of his attempt to publish his first novel *The Poor Man and the Lady* (later subtitled *By the Poor Man*) in 1868. There exists an epistolary narrative ironically related to the text itself. In a pressing letter to the publisher, Alexander Macmillan, Hardy glosses his work as dealing satirically with 'discussions on the questions of manners, rising in the world' (*Letters*, vol.1, p.7). He assumes that 'the upper classes of society' (which he does not distinguish from the middle) will accept criticism if 'painted by a comparative outsider'. Comparative presumably because caste and talent elevate him. Macmillan, in reply, magisterially puts down the upstart, telling Hardy that '. . . nothing could justify such a wholesale blackening of a class but large and intimate knowledge of it'. Thackeray, as an insider, could get away with it, but, Macmillan adds, 'you *"mean mischief"* ' (Millgate, 1982, p.110). Hardy is not allowed in even as a licensed fool; he is not a 'comparative' outsider, just an outsider.

When social class is involved, as so often in the early novels, these two conflicting views of society are in operation. The result is a confusion of optative and actual for both the narrators and those male characters concerned. To speak of the location in this context is to speak of a state of mind: Hardy's narrators,

unlike Gaskell's, perceive themselves as originating on the wrong
side of the social divide but are convinced (as he was when
writing to Macmillan) that by delivering a literary text they have
crossed it. The uncertainty that results from this ambiguous
position produces resentful generalisations against the Gaskell
'us – them' system. So, in *Desperate Remedies* when Cytherea,
as Miss Aldclyffe's companion, is treated with frigid indifference
by two 'gentleman-farmers' wives' their behaviour elicits the tart
comment that: 'A person who socially is nothing is thought less
of by people who are not much than by those who are a great
deal.' (*Desperate Remedies*, p.139.) Similarly, Miss Aldclyffe's
treatment of Springrove is charted from precisely the same
position of social nothingness by one who has evolved into a
species valuable enough to move elsewhere:

> Like a good many others in her position, [she] had plainly not
> realized that a son of her tenant and inferior could have become an
> educated man, who had learnt to feel his individuality, to view
> society from a Bohemian standpoint . . . and that hence he had all
> a developed man's unorthodox opinion about the subordination of
> classes. (*Ibid*. p.212.)

The recognition of this narratorial complaint about her view
as showing a 'Bohemian' and erratic standpoint implies the
simultaneous application of two contradictory views of society.
It is likely that this ambiguous vision of social class was first
captured in *The Poor Man and the Lady* (unpublished in full)
and transferred by textual cannibalism into *Desperate Remedies*,
Under the Greenwood Tree and *A Pair of Blue Eyes*. In the
fragment of the first novel published in 1878, with the ironic
title *An Indiscretion in the Life of an Heiress*, the hero, Egbert
Mayne (earlier Strong, ?'hardy'), a school teacher aspiring
hopelessly to marry the aristocratic Geraldine Allenville, initiates
the paradigm: a figure whose viewpoint and sensibilities parallel
those of the narrator that I have described above, since he is
both poor man and literary artist. The two together provide
those necessary trajectories through events which underwrite the
validity of their aspirations, the rightness of their negative
feelings. Mayne is matched in *A Pair of Blue Eyes* by Stephen
Smith, son of a mason, who has the marginally artistic job of

architect's assistant and is rejected by the clerical father of Elfride Swancourt; and by Swithin St Cleeve in *Two on a Tower*, a brilliant astronomer and the son of a peasant mother, despised as a suitor for Lady Constantine by her brother, Louis. Though the perceived degree of social inferiority and of talent varies, other men are generically linked to this central figure: Edward Springrove, Gabriel Oak (also né Strong), Christopher Julian, Diggory Venn, and George Somerset in *A Laodicean* (as well, of course, as Jude Fawley).

The first three men, and to a lesser extent the others, all encounter an external constraint similar to that imposed on women: their social value is determined for society by the category to which they are seen by upper-class characters primarily to belong – a 'low' social class. This disvaluing of the individual on grounds of class is prominent in *An Indiscretion* where the whole text turns on that subject. Geraldine reports a conversation with her father about her humble lover: 'I said . . . "suppose a man should love me very much, would you mind my being acquainted with him if he were a very worthy man?" "That depends upon his rank and circumstances," he said.' (*An Indiscretion*, p.77.) When Stephen Smith, now known as a mason's son, asks Elfride's father for an interview he is answered similarly: 'Certainly. Though antecedently it does not seem possible that there can be anything of the nature of private business between us.' (*A Pair of Blue Eyes*, p.102.) And Swancourt reacts to Elfride's confession of love equally dismissively: 'Foh! A fine story. It is not enough that I have been deluded by having him here – the son of one of my village peasants, – but now I am to make him my son-in-law! Heavens above us, are you mad, Elfride?' (*Ibid.* p.104.) Even Viviette Constantine finds it socially impossible when St Cleeve asks to marry her: 'Lady Constantine was so agitated at the unexpected boldness of such a proposal from one hitherto so boyish and deferential that she sank into the observing-chair.' She feels she dare not accept; and offers to wait until his name is 'fairly well known', when the match would be less shocking (*Two on a Tower*, p.121).

These constraints are recognised by the victims as inescapable facts. Mayne's recurrent thought, cast in contradictorily decorous terms, is 'What a vast gulf lay between that lady and himself, what a troublesome world it was to live in where such divisions could exist, and how painful was the evil when a man of his unequal history was possessed of a keen susceptibility.' (*An Indiscretion*, p.30) He even accepts that the only 'absolutely honest road' to Geraldine's 'sphere' is 'to try to rise to her level by years of sheer exertion' (*ibid*. p.73). Smith, when rejected by Elfride's father, promises to 'make a fortune, and come to you' (*A Pair of Blue Eyes*, p.115). Similarly St Cleeve combines knowing his place with hopeful aspirations based on his talent. Again with due decorum in address he asks her for permission to marry her, not consent: 'Dear Lady Constantine, allow me to marry you . . . I mean, marry you quite privately. . . . I know that in my present position you could not possibly acknowledge me as husband publicly.' (*Two on a Tower*, pp.120–1.) He accepts the implication of her desire to wait for his fame: 'But I cannot be famous unless I strive, and this distracting condition prevents all striving.' (*Ibid*. p.121.)

Like women in the early novels Swithin is here internalising the category-based disvaluing of himself; and the other men do the same. Mayne seeing Geraldine on her home ground is awed into a state of mind that offers a strange metamorphosis of the prevailing view of a wife as a chattel: 'He . . . wished that he might own her, not exactly as a wife, but as a being superior to himself – in the sense in which a servant may be said to own a master.' (*Ibid*. p.32.) He wishes to own her, then, only as a wife might effectively own a husband. Stephen's self-disvaluing parallels this when his down-to-earth mother wonders whether Elfride is good enough for him: 'Why to marry her would be the great blessing of my life – socially and practically, as well as in other respects. No such good fortune as that I'm afraid; she's too far above me. Her family doesn't want such country lads as I in it.' (*A Pair of Blue Eyes*, p.110.)

But the acceptance of these class-based limits is seen by the narrator to conflict recurrently with the male sense of self, as the limits of womanliness conflict with the female sense of self in Cytherea, Elfride and Bathsheba, and supremely Ethelberta. This is most evident in *An Indiscretion* where Mayne's self-abasement is matched by an equal degree of resentment, based on the double wound to his self-esteem delivered by those who ignore his 'caste' as a schoolmaster and who block his entry, by marriage, into the upper classes. Though at times he, as I have shown, assents to the system, he resents the need to acquire value, a need only on the presumption of his natural unworthiness: 'That the habits of men should be so subversive of the law of nature as to indicate that he was not worthy to marry a woman whose own instincts said that he was worthy, was a great anomaly, he thought, with some rebelliousness.' (*An Indiscretion*, p.73.) Stephen Smith's complaisance is likewise splintered by Knight's patronising excuse that he still seems 'too much of a boy' for the courtesy of an introduction to Elfride. Conscious of Elfride's infidelity to himself, Smith is stirred to 'dim bitterness': 'You should have said that I seemed still the rural builder's son I am, and hence unfit subject for the ceremony of introductions.' (*A Pair of Blue Eyes*, p.268.) The narrator supports his assumptions (*ibid.* p.248) that social class is a factor in Elfride's defection, with a social generalisation similar to the infamous ones about women's nature:

> Few women of old family can be thoroughly taught that a fine soul may wear a smock-frock, and an admittedly common man in one is but a worm in their eyes. John Smith's rough hands and clothes, his wife's speeches, the necessary narrowness of their ways, being constantly under Elfride's notice, were not without their deflecting influence. (*Ibid.* p.258.)

Swithin, coerced into confirmation by Viviette, endures their public distance during the ceremony but is resentful of her vivacious departure with the bishop and other social dignitaries. Like Mayne and Smith he equivocates about his resentment: 'Not that he felt much jealousy of her situation . . . His momentary doubt was of his own strength to achieve sufficiently high things to render him, in relation to her, other than a patronized young favourite, whom she had married at an immense sacrifice of position.' (*Two on a Tower*, p.170.)

Because for Hardy, at this stage, the socially oppressed was characteristically male, the women in the three novels under discussion are for part of the time seen as upper-class oppressors. This is so throughout *An Indiscretion* and in the earlier parts of

A Pair of Blue Eyes and *Two on a Tower*. Geraldine in particular is the instrument of class cruelty. She experiences the 'horrid thought' of how Mayne's habits and her own differ, how their contrasting positions cannot be reconciled.

> There was no doubt about their being lovers . . . and, in spite of Geraldine's warm and unreflecting impulses, a sense of how little Egbert was accustomed to what is called society, and the polite forms which constant usage had almost made nature with her, would rise on occasion, and rob her of many an otherwise pleasant minute. When any little occurrence had brought this into more prominence than usual, Egbert would go away . . . and be kept awake a great part of the night by the distress of mind such a recognition brought upon him. How their intimacy would end, in what uneasiness, yearning, and misery, he could not guess. As for picturing a future of happiness with her by his side there was not ground enough . . . Thus they mutually oppressed each other even while they loved. (*An Indiscretion*, pp.67–8.)

The reality of this oppression from Egbert's side is illustrated by the fact that Geraldine continues to let him call her 'Madame'. Though it slips from a term of social respect to a 'soft pet sound', he winces at its implications: 'He often wondered . . . at the strange condition of a girl's heart which could allow so much in reality, and at the same time permit the existence of a little barrier such as that; how the keen intelligent mind of woman could be ever so slightly hoodwinked by a sound.' (*Ibid.* pp.70–1.)

Elfride subjects Stephen to the same kind of humiliation through the trivial over his handling of the chess pieces. She becomes an insulting Estella confronting a Pip, in what may be her pompously phrased reaction: 'Antecedently she would have supposed that the same performance must be gone through by all players in the same manner; she was taught by his differing action that all ordinary players, who learn the game by sight, unconsciously touch the men in a stereotyped way.' (*A Pair of Blue Eyes*, p.74.) After commenting on the 'indescribable oddness' of his method, she further humiliates him by allowing him to win and then to realise what she has done. For a moment she even relishes this unaccustomed reversal of gender roles which is later to be turned back upon her.

Similarly, it is Viviette who, by insisting on a clandestine marriage, lays Swithin open to a rebuke from the bishop for supposed sexual immorality, a charge 'tremendously' painful to him through 'the double embarrassment arising from misapprehended ethics and inability to set matters right' (*Two on a Tower*, p.186). Despite his humiliation, Viviette still refuses to make the marriage public. How could she, asks the narrator ironically, on Swithin's behalf, 'When her feeling had been cautiously fed and developed by her brother Louis's unvarnished exhibition of Swithin's material position in the eyes of the world?' (*Ibid*. p.198.)

Clearly the experience of humiliation and disvaluing that these men undergo is exacerbated by the loss of normal male dominance. But paradoxically the recognition of this fact seems to open the narrator's eyes to the unjust asymmetry of the conventional power relationship between men and women. In *Two on a Tower* he explores to the fullest extent the perceptions that Mayne, Smith, St Cleeve, Cytherea, Elfride, Bathsheba and others share. It is Viviette who undergoes them in an extreme form after reading a letter from St Cleeve's uncle cynically warning him against her. She is afraid he will be infected with this hostile view:

The humiliation of such a possibility was almost too much to endure; the mortification – she had known nothing like it till now. But this was not all. There succeeded a feeling in comparison with which resentment and mortification were happy moods – a miserable conviction that this old man . . . was not altogether wrong in his speaking; that he was only half wrong; that he was, perhaps, virtually right. Only those persons who are by nature affected with that ready esteem for others' positions which induces an undervaluing of their own, fully experience the deep smart of such convictions against self – the wish for annihilation that is engendered in the moment of despair . . . (*Ibid*. p.230.)

In experiences like these the lives of poor men (as Hardy conceives them) and of even upper-class women intersect. From the theoretical confusion emerges the recognition for the narrator that the two are not entirely discrete categories. An alternative division of semantic space is possible in which gender boundaries are not always significant; humiliation transcends them and so may other things. Consequently woman is now perceived repeatedly as a metaphor for that poor man whose class values, resentments and aspirations the narrator stresses. The equation of the two is radically subversive of the womanly ideal and of the conventional power relationship. I shall now trace these metaphors through the early novels.

A glimmer of possible equivalence is infiltrated into the consciousness of even Edward Springrove under the pressure of guilty depression: 'Echoes of himself . . . he now and then found. Sometimes they were men, sometimes women . . .' The narrator elaborates in contradiction of his own misogynistic generalisations: 'For in spite of a fashion which pervades the whole community at the present day – the habit of exclaiming that woman is not undeveloped man, but diverse, the fact remains that, after all, women are Mankind, and that in many of the sentiments of life the difference of sex is but a difference of degree' (*Desperate Remedies*, p.193.) But it is Stephen Smith who reveals the full equation to the narrator, when his sense of inferiority floods humiliatingly over him at the time of Swancourt's dismissive rejection: 'Quickly acquiring any kind of knowledge he saw around him, and having a plastic adaptability more common in woman than in man, he changed colour like a chameleon as the society he found himself in assumed a higher and more artificial tone' (*A Pair of Blue Eyes*, p.113). His absorption of the class prejudices which condemn him mirrors precisely the uneasy acceptance of standards of womanliness by Cytherea, Elfride and Bathsheba, which suffuse them with anxiety, insecurity and self-doubt.

When circumstances turn St Cleeve from a masterful and 'promising young physicist' to the 'common-place inamorato' of a titled woman, he is left waiting 'helplessly as a girl for a chance of encountering her' (*Two on a Tower*, pp.112–13). This is merely his belated recognition of a reversal of gender already evident to the narrator. Ethelberta's more conscious assumption of a masculine role has a similar effect on the impoverished music teacher, Christopher Julian. This is unexpected; he has seemed the one prepared to stoop to conquer. The discovery of Ethelberta's lowly origin has been 'a positive pleasure to one whose faith in society had departed with his own social ruin' (*The Hand of Ethelberta*, p.118). But, after her success as a public performer, he finds himself swamped, woman-like, with an 'unmanageable excess of feeling', which contrasts with her control. Though he assumes that it is only in what he thinks of as 'little things' that 'their sexes were thus reversed', he still recognises that: 'It was always so, always had been so, always would be so, at these meetings of theirs: she was immeasurably the stronger; and the deep-eyed young man fancied, in the chagrin which the perception of this difference always bred in him, that she triumphed in her superior control.' (*Ibid.* pp.132–3.) This powerlessness is all too familiar to women in the early novels; and it is powerlessness that Showalter sees as the root of the metaphor in its central use, later, in *The Mayor of Casterbridge*. When Henchard is overcome by womanly sentiments of 'shame and self-reproach', after his brutal physical attack on Farfrae, the narrator comments: 'So thoroughly subdued was he that he remained on the sacks in a crouching attitude, unusual for a man, and for such a man. Its womanliness sat tragically on the figure of so stern a piece of virility.' (*The Mayor of Casterbridge*, p.279.) Showalter interprets this as the culmination of 'a pilgrimage of "unmanning" which is a movement towards both self-discovery and tragic vulnerability' (Kramer, 1979, p.102). I read it also as one amongst a string of metaphors in which the startling equivalence of the two sexes undermines Spencerian and essentialist accounts of women.

This seems to be borne out by the handling of the third sign, *the artist*. Originally in what may be regarded as the first novel, *An Indiscretion*, it is used for a male writer, Egbert Mayne, father of the other gifted men in the early texts. He represents a specifically nineteenth century modification of the artist as outsider, found for instance in Gissing: one pressurised in a consumerist society by manifestations of consumer demands. The summary of Mayne's five years of literary life is an account of a struggle for success in the market place:

It had been drive, drive from month to month; no rest, nothing but effort. He had progressed from newspaper work to criticism, from criticism to independent composition of a mild order, from the latter to the publication of a book which nobody ever heard of, and from this to the publication of a work of really sterling merit, which appeared anonymously. (*An Indiscretion*, p.81.)

Critically the interest this book arouses is focused on curiosity about his name, something natural at a time when it would be judged quite differently if it could be attached to the name of an already successful and well-paid author. Built into this account, and evidently shared by the narrator, is a sense of 'injured merit', based on dislike of a public that is lion-hunting and trivialising. The public is also a task-master that tends to corrupt those like Mayne, who try to satisfy it: 'His original fondness for art, literature, and science, was getting quenched by his slowly increasing habit of looking upon each and all of these as machinery wherewith to effect a purpose.' (*Ibid*. p.82.) The 'perpetual strain' eventually causes him to retire to the country to free himself from the 'intricate web of effort' that holds him trapped (*ibid*. pp.99–100).

Mayne's brief literary career does not extend to include the enhanced humiliation created by the reviewing methods that helped to enforce the constraints imposed by current methods of publication and circulation in the supposed interests of the consumer. The method frequently used was to replace the text by the author and subject him to personal attack and disvaluing. So, for instance, the sensational nature of *Desperate Remedies* led a reviewer in *The Spectator* in 1871 to focus on its anonymous publication as better than disgrace for a named author: 'By all means let him bury the secret in the profoundest depths of his own heart, out of reach, if possible, of his own consciousness.' (Millgate, 1982, p.133.) In Hardy himself and presumably others the distress caused by such personal attacks was exacerbated by a sensitivity which remained excruciatingly sharp. His reaction to *The Spectator* review was for a time to wish himself dead. Later financial success was no balm, after the publication of *Tess*, to a feeling that he could not enter his London club for fear of meeting one particularly hostile critic (*ibid*. p.319). A reference in *The World* in 1897 describing him as having 'once more afforded a dismayed and disgusted public the depressing spectacle of genius on the down grade' caused pain measurable by the venom of his reaction in a private notebook: 'What foul cess pits some men's minds must be, and what a night-cart would be required to empty them!' (*Ibid*. pp.382–3.) As late as 1924 he reacted to George Moore's attack on his style and reputation by reviving a reference to him as a 'putrid literary hermaphrodite' (*ibid*. p.553).

Yet as with Mayne there is an extent to which writers allowed themselves to be manipulated by the consumerist machine. This is evident in Hardy's disingenuous defences of many works including *Desperate Remedies* and *Two on a Tower*, which were rightly judged as sexually explicit or unconventional by prevailing standards. More than this, he allowed himself to be led by the praise of peripheral rustic elements in *Desperate Remedies* to bring next to the publishers a pastoral story, *Under the Greenwood Tree*. The bowdlerising of later novels for serial publication, similarly determined by external constraints, was not entirely erased by the definitive Wessex Edition of 1912–14. The entrapment is partly internal as well as external. In this respect the alienated artist of the period differs from earlier and later variations where, essentially, artistic integrity is usually preserved.

But the second appearance in Hardy's novels of a sign drawing on the peculiarly Victorian figure of the artist–writer is no longer male. This is Elfride in *A Pair of Blue Eyes*; and she is followed by Ethelberta. In these texts an astonishing transposition has taken place: it is women who now subsume the condition of the artist into their own, not vice versa (as with the poor man). The artist-writer is the vehicle of a metaphor that questions the conventional signification of *woman/womanly/womanliness*. It is Elfride's writing that she offers as her raison d'être when her new stepmother asks, before Knight appears, what she finds to do with herself: '. . . I read, and I write a little' (*A Pair of Blue Eyes*, p.142). The publication of her 'Romance of Lyonesse' under (naturally) a male pseudonym, Ernest Field, draws Knight's fire as a reviewer. The irrelevant preoccupation with identity complained of by Mayne (and reflected in the review of *Desperate Remedies*) is now carried to extremes. With heavy-handed irony Knight elaborates on how expectations of literary pleasure were shattered at finding himself not in the text but 'in the hands of some young lady, hardly arrived at years of discretion, to judge by the silly device it has been thought worth while to adopt on the title-page, with the idea of disguising her sex.' (*Ibid*. p.162.) The text has attempted to conceal its gender

and once the disguise has been stripped away it is considered to
be dismantled: it is discredited by being manifestly a silly young
female. Knight writes it down as he writes down Elfride's person
in his notebook entry. To revive the authentic gender he praises
the womanly parts of the text, those best suited to female
intelligence:

> We are far from altogether disparaging the author's powers. She has
> a certain versatility that enables her to use with effect a style of
> narration peculiar to herself, which may be called a murmuring of
> delicate emotional trifles, the particular gift of those to whom the
> social sympathies of a peaceful time are as daily food. Hence, where
> matters of domestic experience, and the natural touches which make
> people real, can be introduced without anachronisms too striking,
> she is occasionally felicitous; and upon the whole we feel justified
> in saying that the book will bear looking into for the sake of those
> portions which have nothing whatever to do with the story. (*Ibid.*
> p.163.)

There is a marked parallel, noted by Richard Taylor in *The
Neglected Hardy* (Taylor, 1982, p.45) between this and the
wounding reviews of *Desperate Remedies* praising those rustic
elements in the text which, also, have 'nothing . . . to do with
the story'. In both the authors are relegated to appropriately
marginal areas of experience for them as either a low-born rustic
or a woman.

Knight's review, as Mrs Swancourt recognises, polishes off
Elfride as a writer, turns her back into the woman she had
foolishly tried to escape from. As 'the Lady' in the early part of
the novel she has tormented the underling, Stephen Smith; now
she takes over from him the role of the tormented when Knight
ousts him as her lover. From being the oppressor, now with no
other identity than that of being female she becomes the
oppressed, a fact recognised as I have shown in Chapter 2, by
the narrator. The analogy between her and Stephen is underlined
when Knight plays out his dominance in games of chess as
Elfride played out hers earlier with Stephen. Knight, moreover,
would willingly go further as a critic of women as writers and
adjure that silence and erasure which the *Spectator* reviewer
suggested for the (anonymous) Hardy when it urged him to
disappear from his own consciousness. He tells Elfride to her

face: 'That a young woman has taken to writing is not by any means the best thing to hear about her.' She inevitably, both as woman and writer, must find out what her consumer demands:

> 'What is the best?' . . .
> 'I suppose to hear that she has married.' . . .
> 'And what when she has been married?' . . .
> 'Then to hear no more about her.' (*A Pair of Blue Eyes*, p.171.)

There is similar disparagement of the other woman, Ethelberta, who figures startlingly in the early novels as a writer. Dinner-table discussion of her published verses, shielded under the anonymity of *Metres by E*, soon reveals again that the first consideration in literary assessment is her identity, particularly her gender. Appraisal of her as a woman is its focus, with her temperament and virtue in excited question.

> 'She is rather warm in her assumed character'. 'That's a sign of her actual coldness; she lets off her feeling in theoretic grooves, and there is sure to be none left for practical ones.' . . . 'O, I don't mean to call her warmth of feeling a vice or virtue exactly – ' (*The Hand of Ethelberta*, p.75.)

In her case the personal criticism is reductively sexual whether it comes from men or women. The men are titillated by the self-exposure of publication and the women are shocked at its unwomanliness: '"I am sure, when I was at the ardent age," said the mistress of the house ". . . I could no more have printed such emotions and made them public than I could have helped privately feeling them."' (*Ibid.* p.76.) Such silencing is regarded by Ethelberta's less sophisticated mother-in-law, Lady Petherwin, as the only natural course. As a widow Elfride should have left her verses unwritten as a mark of respect; as a woman, she should have suppressed them rather than reveal an anarchical female subconscious that would disgrace her sex: 'Really, one would imagine that women wrote their books during those dreams in which people have no moral sense to see how improper some, even virtuous, ladies become when they get into print.' (*A Pair of Blue Eyes*, p.97.) Ethelberta escapes from her humiliation as an artist by achieving worldly success and from her humiliation as a woman by assuming a masculine control of events. I have dealt with the significance of her story in Chapter 3: it creates a figurative (and superficial) resolution of the problem of oppression. The still-present difficulty of relating class and gender oppression theoretically was later again circumvented by Hardy when he allowed a woman to stand for those oppressed because of their 'low' class. In this way he made Tess, and even Sue to an extent, double victims: it is poverty and wretchedness that facilitate their oppression as women. After the appearance of Ethelberta as the representative disvalued artist, that particular sign disappears from his language. The next (and last) artist that Hardy depicted was Jocelyn Pearston/Pierston in *The Well-Beloved*, who is viewed with satirical detachment. What I have been concerned to demonstrate in this chapter, however, is how the complex equation of signs described above prepares for that shift in the signification of *woman* that I shall discuss next.

CHAPTER FIVE

Women as Signs in the Later Novels

By the 1880s many of the social limitations which paradoxically had provided the material coded into literary stereotypes of 'ideal' womanhood had changed. The most striking of these changes were modifications of the negatives that had constructed a married woman's legal position; such negatives had been encoded as Ruskin's radiant positives. A married woman did not before that decade, as a feme covert, legally exist; hence her incapacity in dissolving a marriage. The Divorce Act of 1857 meant that whereas a husband could use adultery alone as adequate grounds, a wife needed some aggravation in the form of incest, bigamy, cruelty or desertion. But the Matrimonial Causes Act of 1884 enacted that desertion (as the necessary aggravation of adultery) could be equated with a husband's refusal to obey an order for the restitution of conjugal rights. The wife of such an offender could therefore, after 1884, obtain a divorce without waiting two years to prove desertion. A married woman was also becoming more of a legal person in relation to her rights over children, since the Custody of Infants Act of 1873 gave a mother rights in certain circumstances to children up to the age of 16 rather than 7. She also became enough of a person to have some claim to her own property. The Married Woman's Property Act of 1870 protected her wages and earnings and extended the range of her separate estate. The identically named Act of 1882 went further: wives could now acquire, hold and dispose of any real or personal property as their own, exactly like the unmarried. Married women by now were half-persons.

The attempted reversal of this radical process by the enshrining of the double-standard in the Contagious Diseases Acts (designed for the hygienic supervision of prostitutes) was blocked by Josephine Butler. She led the campaign culminating in the Repeal of 1883, and attacked the hypocrisy of the double standard head-on:

> It is manifest that on all sides it begins to be felt that the principle is to be decided whether male profligacy, at the expense of women, is to be condoned, excused, and darkly perpetrated, or to be sternly condemned and pertinaciously resisted . . . . The evil we oppose is rooted in a *yet more cruel negation of human brotherhood, and a more immoral violation of the principle of liberty* [than slavery]. (Helsinger, 1983, vol.2, p.163.)

At the same time women's sphere widened as the enabling force of proper education spread. From 1872 secondary schools for girls developed on the model of the North London Collegiate School (1850) and Cheltenham (1853). This was gradually followed by permission for women to sit as candidates for the Tripos examination at Cambridge in 1870; in Honour Schools at Oxford from 1872; and in degree examinations at Manchester and London in 1880. Women like Elizabeth Garrett Anderson began to press for entry into the medical profession; and she achieved it by a devious route in 1866 via the Society of Apothecaries.

But an improving legal status did not displace the traditional signification of woman any more than a change in other referents (e.g., *ship*) or the knowledge of them (e.g., *atom*) directly causes semantic shift. The meanings of *woman/hood/ly* as signs served to reinforce the real and imaginary relation to the world which is ideology. The connection between language and referent is not direct: cigarette-smoking in the advertising code still speaks of sophistication, allure and athletic vigour long after the link with lung cancer has been established in reality. No doubt a recoding is being prepared for, but the change in an understanding of cigarette-smoking in the real world cannot alone effect it. In the same way no doubt the intelligent and articulate who battled for the limited improvements in the status of women, described above, prepared the way for a change in literary language by creating new material to draw on. Events could do no more and might simply have resulted in a more sophisticated coding of traditional 'womanliness'.

Ironically a shift from the all embracing womanly ideal was disapprovingly anticipated as early as 1867 by that autonomous woman, Margaret Oliphant, who supported three children and at least two inadequate male relatives by her writing. She notices the bridgehead made by sensation novels like *Lady Audley's Secret* (Braddon, 1862) which mould women, morally speaking, 'on the model of men' (Helsinger, 1983, vol.3, p.141). She foresees, in terms that encapsulate what an ideological signification is, a new sign offered to English girl readers: 'intense appreciation of flesh and blood . . . eagerness of physical sensation . . . is offered to them *not only as the portrait of their own state of mind, but as their amusement and mental food.*' (*Ibid.* p.140, my emphasis.) The actual beginnings of a semantic shift in the general signification of woman I see as that described in my fourth chapter as taking place in Hardy's early novels. It presumably also took place elsewhere, since language is public property and no individual can effect a change single-handed, though she may apparently initiate it. Fortunately at this time such a change was explicitly discussed very widely in literary reviews and elsewhere in other periodicals. Attention was directed to the linguistic constraints that had for decades existed in the novel: a stated set of signs, restricted narrative patterns, a specified semantic range. The literary debate on the nature and duties of women, now thoroughly destabilised by events as well as arguments, was replaced by one which ran through the seventies, eighties and nineties on these topics. The contexts in which novelistic language was scrutinised were three: the anomalous sensation novels of the 1860s and 1870s; the tyranny of the circulating libraries; and the assessment of French 'realist' writers such as Flaubert and Zola.

The first of these, the 'fast' novels of those like Mary Braddon and Wilkie Collins, were the predictable results of pressure built up by the exclusion from serious fiction of sexual matters. The potency acquired from taboo meant that adultery, divorce and bigamy became the staples of such works. But their radicalism is compromised by the combination of sensational events with a priggish register. A two-faced reader is inscribed – ignorant, innocent and high-minded – who wishes to know in detail about lurid stories only in order to feel the appropriate surges of moral indignation. As one critic wrote approvingly: 'All the crime is done under proper reprobation, and yet the writer and readers have all the benefit of the crime.' (*Ibid*. vol.3, p.131.) Lady Audley in Braddon's *Lady Audley's Secret* (Braddon, 1862) is a bigamist and only through moral luck not a murderer. The contrast between her dark deeds and the 'unearthly glitter of her beauty' is gloated over (Braddon, p.340). Once past the boundary between innocence and guilt she becomes demoniac in her evil. This kind of story is far removed from Dickens and Trollope and other mainstream writers, but it does establish a narrow bridgehead in new semantic territory which Hardy quickly extended in *Desperate Remedies*. 'Fast' fiction provoked of course much critical discussion of its own acceptability. Opponents attacked the mere inclusion of taboo material. 'In drawing her [Lady Lucy Audley], the authoress may have intended to portray a female Mephistopheles; but, if so, she should have known that a woman cannot fill such a part.' (Helsinger, 1983, vol.3, p.127.)

But the opportunity offered by public discussion of the new subjects in fiction was seized by those critics who wished to extend the novel. Securing their defences by pointing out that sinners always suffer in these texts, liberals were able to argue for an extension in semantic range:

> That sense of propriety which is satisfied by simply pretending that we do not see and hear things which no human precaution can shut out from our eyes and ears, is worthy of nothing but contempt.
> . . . We would not teach women that they are mere puppets of man's passion, soulless creatures for whom, as for children, an absence of all individual responsibility may be claimed. (Justin MacCarthy cited in Helsinger, 1983, vol.3, p.129.)

In the two other topics which involved the scrutiny of novelistic constraints several major novelists were themselves involved. The pressure for release from Mudie's tyranny focused on the particular reader whom novelists were instructed to inscribe in their work, as pictorial artists were to inscribe a particular eye. The annual Royal Academy exhibition in 1877 stimulated Henry

James to complain of this reader/eye: 'Here, as throughout the field of English art and letters, the influence of the "young person" and her sensitive cheek is perceived to prevail.' (Jones, 1985, p.110.)

George Moore, however, became the standard bearer for novelists against 'Literature at Nurse, or Circulating Morals' (first published 1885). Though mainly concerned with the inconsistencies of Mudie's library in accepting sensation novels, he castigates the tyrannical censorship exerted through an insistence on the appropriateness of novels as reading matter for ignorant young girls. Moore's method of attack is mainly derision not argument:

> Into this nursery none can enter except in baby clothes; and the task of discriminating between a divided skirt and a pair of trousers is performed by the librarian. Deftly his fingers lift skirt and under-skirt, and if the examination proves satisfactory the sometimes decently attired dolls are packed in tin-cornered boxes, and scattered through every drawing-room in the kingdom, to be in rocking-chairs fingered and fondled by the 'young person' until she longs for some newer fashion in literary frills and furbelows. Mudie is the law we labour after; the suffrage of young women we are supposed to gain: the paradise of the English novelist is in the school-room. (Moore in Coustillas, 1976, pp.18–19.)

But though Moore saw himself as the David to Mudie's Goliath he is trapped into a recognition of conventional standards that delivers him bound to Mrs Grundy: 'The close analysis of a passion has no attraction for the young girl. When she is seduced through the influence of a novel, it is by a romantic story, the action of which is laid outside the limits of her experience.' (*Ibid*. p.22.) This pattern of entrapment recurs, as I shall show, in both areas of the debate where novelists concern themselves.

French novels had already extended the semantic map at an early date: Flaubert's *Madame Bovary* (1857) for instance was published in 1857 and produced an English offspring in Mary Braddon's sensation novel, *The Doctor's Wife* (Braddon, 1864). English novelists saw in this extension a means of leverage on the central issue of whether to dispense with the inscribed young girl and treat sexual relationships as centrally and as naturalistically as French writers had done. In this context there appeared three symposia in *The New Review* 1890–1, which serve to illustrate the debate: 'Candour in English Fiction', 'The Science of Fiction' and 'The Science of Criticism'. Hardy contributed to the first two, Henry James to the third, though his major contributions on the subject are found elsewhere.

Both, like Moore, urge unlimited exploration on artistic grounds; but both, in doing so, recreate like him an entrapment reminiscent both of the reforming side in the debate on women's nature and also of women in fiction. As usual the framework for the argument was set by those who defended the literary status quo. Walter Besant in an article preceding Hardy's in 'Candour in English Fiction' appears to take a liberal view that fiction should deal with 'every passion, every emotion' and that every artist is 'absolutely free' (Besant, *The New Review*, 2, 1890, p.6), but he tells how 'Average Opinion' imposes restraints which imply that 'Modern society is based upon the unit of the family. The family tie means, absolutely, that the man and the woman are indissolubly united and can only be parted by the shame and disgrace of one or the other.' (*Ibid*. p.7.) He sees 'Average Opinion', a Jamesian *bête noire*, embodied in the power of the circulating libraries and is somewhat equivocal about authors needing to choose between restricting their pencils or their purses. Finally he comes out: 'Love free and disobedient' is outside the social pale and 'is destructive of the very basis of society' (*ibid*. p.9).

The truth (or otherwise) of this assumption that naturalistic literature is socially as well as morally subversive is not directly confronted by the major novelists themselves in the discussion, but it bedevils them. Henry James had also wanted the novelist to be perfectly free to include whatever he chooses: '. . . the good health of an art which undertakes so immediately to reproduce life must demand that it be perfectly free. It lives upon exercise and the very meaning of exercise is freedom.' (James, *Partial Portraits*, 1888, p.384). Though he claims such freedom here in 'The Art of Fiction', the conventional constraints emerge as, in the same essay, he reverts to what Vivien Jones calls 'a deep-seated prudery' that distorts his moral aesthetic (Jones, 1985, p.65). He assumes that 'the young aspirant in the

line of fiction . . . will do nothing without taste, for in that case
his freedom would be of little use to him' (James, *Partial
Portraits*, 1888, p.399). Similarly in his public utterance in *The
New Review* Hardy also repeats the familiar pattern, in spite of
his personal stress on the scientific nature of the new inclusiveness.
He appears to speak without restraint:

> conscientious fiction alone it is which can excite a reflective and
> abiding interest in the minds of thoughtful readers . . . famishing
> for accuracy. . . . Life being a physiological fact, its honest portrayal
> must be largely concerned with . . . the relations of the sexes. . . .
> To this expansion English society opposes a well-nigh insuperable
> bar. (Orel, 1967, pp. 127–8.)

He sees English prudery and hypocritical commercialism exclud-
ing subjects that have been, since ancient times, the basis of
great literature. Most strikingly he declares that: 'The crash of
broken commandments is as necessary an accompaniment to the
catastrophe of a tragedy as the noise of drum and cymbals to a
triumphal march.' (*Ibid.* p.129.) He rightly thinks that existing
censorship inhibits accounts which might show the breaking of
the first, third, and seventh (*ibid.* p.129).

But Hardy and other serious male novelists, entrapped by
censorship, are like women of the period. Some of these when
pressing for better education for girls agreed to prevent instruction
from interfering with fertility, as their opponents claimed it
would, though this contradicted the basis of their argument.
Similarly Hardy tries to placate critics he has just declared
irrelevant: he doubles back on himself by apparently accepting
that naturalistic accounts of sexual relationships should be
censored for moral subversiveness. They should not and would
not 'exhibit lax views of that purity of life upon which the well-
being of society depends' (Orel, 1967, p.133).

It was, however, Hardy (and others like Moore) who helped
break the constraints against which novelists had fretted in their
critical discussion of what to do in the novel. Already he had
extended the treatment of women's physicality by developing a
sub-erotic register in some early novels. After *Two on a Tower*
(1882), he told a correspondent he determined to get rid of 'the
doll of English fiction', an essential change 'if England is to have

a school of fiction at all' (*Letters*, vol.1, p.250). The new register to which this refers continued to be used and extended into a more fully erotic range in *Tess*. After 1887 he took always the topics, dropped after *Desperate Remedies*, now made familiar by the sensation novels – adultery, marital breakdown, divorce, bigamy, even hinted-at incest, abandoning the false colouring 'best expressed by the regulation finish that "they married and were happy ever after" ' (Orel, 1967, p.127–8).

I now wish to examine the role of women in *The Woodlanders*, *Tess* and *Jude*, to show the evolution of a new set of feminine signs, recodings that are developments as much as innovations: Grace of the womanly, Tess and Arabella of the fallen woman, Sue of the New Woman. These women are all involved in feelings and actions previously excluded by taboo; yet they are not, like Lucy Audley, freaks and beyond the pale. They all make for themselves by a certain autonomy a new meaning, though as yet no descriptive language exists for it. They are seen deviating from the former womanly ideal without moving into the unwomanly category. Hence the preoccupation of males – both narrators and characters – with establishing a reading for them; and hence the contradictions in those readings. The superficial self-contradiction of Hardy the critic (visible also in letters to male, compared with female, correspondents) gives way to the profounder ambivalence of Hardy the novelist that enacts a contemporary confusion felt most strongly by a liberal-minded and sensitive male.

Central to this change is a focus on the issue of women's sexual feelings – read under the old signification as existing only vicariously. Spontaneous sexuality is now, however, an essential characteristic of all four women. With Grace Melbury in *The Woodlanders* it is what undermines the traditional significance of the pure, middle-class girl. Her father reads her as the familiar, delicate, refined and sexless being who will naturally marry Giles, the appropriate husband he has chosen for her. By one of the multiple ironies the choice is dictated by Melbury's wish to expiate his own guilt towards Giles's family. When a new desire to raise her to a class above his own, fitted to her 'womanly mien and manners', brings a new choice of husband, the doctor, Fitzpiers, the commercial nature of the arrangement is made clear: 'If it costs me my life you shall marry well! To-day has shown me that whatever a young woman's niceness, she stands for nothing alone.' (*The Woodlanders*, p.85.) Melbury is gratified at the idea of Grace 'making havoc in the upper classes' (*ibid*. p.149).

She accepts her new suitor as she did the old but her reasons are in this context subversive; the doctor arouses her sexually, stirs her 'indescribably': 'That Fitzpiers acted upon her like a dram, exciting her, throwing her into a novel atmosphere which biased her doings until the influence was over, when she felt something of the nature of regret for the mood she had experienced – could not be told to this worthy couple in words.' (*Ibid*. p.150.)

Significantly the nature of her feelings for Fitzpiers is not grasped by her father, falling as it does outside the area of his expectations for a well-bred, womanly girl: 'She could not explain the subtleties of her feeling as clearly as he could state his opinion, even though she had skill in speech, and her father had none.' (*Ibid*. p.150.) She can only tacitly mean (or, as later, utter her deepest feelings in words of untutored directness). Similarly when she overhears Fitzpiers's reference to his infidelity she reacts in an unwomanly way with silence: 'He expected a scene at breakfast – but she only exhibited an extreme reserve.' (*Ibid*. p.206.) He attributes this to what he had said of regret for this marriage but he misconstrues her as surely as her father does later, when he sees her indifference to Fitzpiers's behaviour: 'Melbury wanted to ask her a dozen questions: did she not feel jealous, was she not indignant . . . "You are very tame and let-alone, I am bound to say," he remarked pointedly.' (*Ibid*. p.207.) Her astonishing reply 'I am what I feel' represents a claim to feel and to mean something individual not covered by the routine generalisations about jealous wives. She is herself surprised at this: 'She was quite sure he was going to Mrs. Charmond. Grace was amazed at the mildness of the anger which the suspicion engendered in her: she was but little excited, and her jealousy was languid even to death.' (*Ibid*. p.191.) She can by the 1895 version put her realisation of Fitzpiers's affair into words of a shattering simplicity to Felice Charmond: 'He's had you! Can it be . . .!' (*Ibid*. p.228.) But she accepts the position to the point of feeling sisterly sympathy with Fitzpiers's old and new

mistresses when they attempt to rush to his sick bed. In this
version she articulates this truth also with laconic irony: 'Wives
all, let's enter together'. The moment of irony passes however
and 'the tears which his possibly critical situation could not bring
to her eyes surged over at the contemplation of these fellow-
women whose relations with him were as close as her own
without its conventionality' (ibid. p.243). 'Tenderness' spreads
over her 'like a dew' and she rejects men's language designed
for the description of such women: 'It was well enough,
conventionally, to address either one of them in the wife's
regulation terms of virtuous sarcasm, as woman, creature, or
thing.' (Ibid. p.243.)

Her 'illicit' love for Giles shows the same sexual dimension as
her infatuation with Fitzpiers and grows more explicit when she
asks him with an 'agonizing seductiveness' (in an addition made
in 1895): 'why don't you do what you want to?' (Ibid. p.270).
The 'long embrace and passionate kiss' that result are something
she looks back on gratefully when the idea of divorce collapses.
Her famous refusal to allow Giles to sleep in the hut where she
shelters after running away from her husband deflects attention
from the extended expression of desire, added in 1895, when
she finally invites him in:

'I want you here! . . . Come to me, dearest! I don't mind what they
say, or what they think of us any more.' (Ibid. p.287; my emphasis
for additions).

None of the men in the novel can construe her definitively.
Her father takes her coolness over the infidelity for lack of spirit,
her agreement in a plan for divorce for daughterly dutifulness.
He has no idea, at that stage, of her love for Giles, let alone its
physicality. Fitzpiers conversely, when told after their separation
to read her relationship with Giles as guilty, takes her for a
fallen woman and is titillated by the idea: 'The man whom
Grace's matrimonial fidelity could not keep faithful was stung
into passionate throbs of interest concerning her by her avowal
of the contrary.' (Ibid. p.307.) Giles resists the idea that she is
physically attracted when she calls him into the hut. He is
womanly on her behalf in rejecting the invitation to an impropriety
that might ruin her reputation; he reads her in the old,

false way. Grace thus presents an insidious and sophisticated development of the expectedly womanly like Elfride, Cytherea, Bathsheba and Viviette. She is an image filling a central place as these women had previously done in the web of meaning, but she is a replacement for the ideal who is disturbing to all around her. Tess, on the other hand, presents an overt attempt to replace a more marginal figure, the fallen woman as sign – exemplified by Fanny and Eustacia – with a positive image:

> Let the truth be told – women do as a rule live through such humiliations, and regain their spirits, and again look about them with an interested eye. While there's life there's hope is a conviction not so entirely unknown to the 'betrayed' as some amiable theorists would have us believe. (*Tess of the D'Urbervilles*, p.151.)

She is an explicitly sexual being, her appearance described with the same directness as Grace's feelings: 'She had . . . a luxuriance of aspect, a fulness of growth, which made her appear more of a woman than she really was.' (*Ibid*. p.56.) This directness was noticed by the hostile reviewer who wrote of this passage: 'The story gains nothing by the reader being let into the secret of the physical attributes which especially fascinated him in Tess. Most people can fill in blanks for themselves, without its being necessary to put the dots on the i's so very plainly; but Mr Hardy leaves little unsaid.' (Cox, 1970, p.189.) The new erotic rhetoric is pinpointed here, though the reviewer might have chosen more extreme examples such as Tess's yawn, or the passage in which Clare studies the curves of her lips: '. . . and now, as they again confronted him, clothed with colour and life, they sent an *aura* over his flesh, a breeze through his nerves, which well-nigh produced a qualm' (*Tess of the D'Urbervilles*, p.213). Perhaps the culmination of this passage in a sneeze was one which the critic shrank from mentioning.

Nor is Tess's sexuality evoked only through others: she is aware of her own 'impassioned nature', and has for some time, perhaps always, 'the invincible instinct towards self-delight' (*ibid*. p.141). Under the shock of Clare's finding her living again with Alec she can assert (according to an insertion made by Hardy in his 1912 copy), with the colloquialism seen to mark these women, what the Clarendon editors call 'the primacy of the sexual instinct' (*ibid*. p.54) by telling him that 'the step back to him was not so great as it seems. He had been as husband to me: you never had!' (*Ibid*. p.514.)

As when confronted with Grace, the males of the novel cannot, with the men's language at their disposal, define and place her. Clare believes he can: ' "she is a dear, dear Tess," he thought to himself, as one deciding on the true construction of a difficult passage.' (*Ibid*. p.309.) From early on he, as well as Alec, imposes the signifying framework of men's language upon her. When Tess resists his wooing it is as though '. . . he had made up his mind that her negatives were, after all, only coyness and youth, startled by the novelty of the proposal' (*ibid*. p.261). He reads her as 'a pure woman' of the approved kind, complementary and powerless: 'Do I realize solemnly enough how utterly and irretrievably this little womanly thing is the creature of my good or bad faith and fortune?' (*Ibid*. p.309.) When he experiences her sexual attractiveness and response he can interpret it in a generalisation of a literary kind that appropriates her in the old way: 'He called her Artemis, Demeter, and other fanciful names' (*ibid*. p.186).

Tess, literally not understanding, resists, asserts her claim to her own identity, and begs 'Call me Tess.' (*Ibid*. p.186.) When he finds she has failed in 'purity' he is astonished: 'She looked absolutely pure. Nature, in her fantastic trickery, had set such a seal of maidenhood upon Tess's countenance that he gazed at her with a stupefied air.' (*Ibid*. p.335.) The only conclusion that the categories of his language allow him to draw is that if she is not 'pure' then she is a fallen woman: 'You were one person: now you are another.' (*Ibid*. p.325.)

This erasure of Tess's identity and its replacement by a Magdalen figure is one resisted by that other interested male, the narrator. He deliberately sets aside the generalised reading of the unmarried mother who is innately wretched:

> If she could have been but just created, to discover herself as a spouseless mother, with no experience of life except as the parent of a nameless child, would the position have caused her to despair? No, she would have taken it calmly, and found pleasures therein.

Most of the misery had been generated by her conventional aspect, and not by her innate sensations. (*Ibid*. p.128.)

He wishes to insist on the recognition of individuality as she changes from a simple girl to a complex woman, 'whom the turbulent experiences of the last year or two had quite failed to demoralize'. He goes still further: 'But for the world's opinion those experiences would have been simply a liberal education.' (*Ibid*. p.139.) But he cannot entirely shake off the language of men even, or perhaps particularly, in his defence. The last minute addition to the novel of the subtitle 'A Pure Woman', though peripheral, deflects attention from meanings that Tess herself conveys, by attempting to rehabilitate her under the old womanly category: she may not look it but she is, he says. This subtitle is a reminder of the unitary generalisations of the early novels. It is again referred to when the narrator says of Clare: 'In considering what Tess was not he overlooked what she was, and forgot that the defective can be more than the entire.' (*Ibid*. p.369.) The antithesis of 'defective' and 'entire' is of course itself a conventional one, and, like 'pure', assesses Tess in inappropriate terms. In his most emotional defences of her this tainted terminology undermines the narrator's account by measuring her against the old norms. He slips back into the familiar terms of early generalisations with the description of the rape–seduction (or more correctly, seduction–rape, as argued in chapter 6) as he muses on: 'why it was that upon this beautiful feminine tissue, sensitive as gossamer, and practically blank as snow as yet, there should have been traced such a coarse pattern as it was doomed to receive . . .' (*Ibid*. p.103).

Thus the narrator's defence of Tess involves his recognition of her sexual nature and, as he sees it, its naturalness; but his reading of that aspect of her is an eccentric one, expressive of bewilderment. Since she is not sexless he construes her as all sex, reaching a description of generic 'woman' which is highly reductive:

She was yawning, and he saw the red interior of her mouth . . . She had stretched one arm so high . . . that he could see its satin delicacy above the sunburn . . . The brim-fulness of her nature breathed from her. It was a moment when a woman's soul is more incarnate than at any other time; when the most spiritual beauty bespeaks itself flesh; and sex takes the outside place in the presentation. (*Ibid.* pp.242–3.)

Tess's own meaning, then, is only fully spoken to the extent that she acts it out in deeds, as the next chapter will show. The narrator's attempts at interpretation evoke the ambiguities of a language in transition. The shifting signification of the fallen, as of the womanly woman, involves problems of perception for those who encounter her.

The alternative account of the same figure in *Jude* gives us in Arabella a fallen woman who refuses to fall; she neither measures nor is measured by old norms. Unlike all her predecessors (including Tess) she is guilt free. It is she who seduces Jude, not the other way round. She reacts to the first sight of him with the now familiar directness of these women, speaking in a 'low, hungry tone of latent sensuousness: I've got him to care for me: Yes! But I want him to more than care for me; I want him to have me – to marry me!' (*Jude the Obscure*, p.73.) She brings about both these events by her skilful game with the egg placed between her breasts to hatch. The narrator does not espouse her cause as he does that of Tess, but because of the pizzle-throwing, the pig-chasing and the pig-killing, her characteristic certainty and energy subvert such conventional accounts. She alone is at ease with her own sexuality, can deal with what is presented as the hideous institution of marriage by ignoring it, and finally survives.

These attempts at replacing old signs with new ones with which in practice they conflict disturbs the whole system of meaning, as did the equation of some males with all women in Chapter 4. So too does the incorporation into *Jude* of a sign already consciously constructed mainly by women writers of the 1880s and 1890s. Though labelled the New Woman, she did not occupy a central position in the field of feminine meaning and so offer a replacement for the womanly woman. She was a marginal as well as a self-conscious formation, a coding of the privileged few: ostentatiously well-read if not well-educated, and high-mindedly opposed to marriage, which was rigidly defined as legal prostitution. Narratorial accounts of such women lack Hardy's early physicality and though their sentiments go beyond the pale there is in the expression of them none of the colloquial directness (even awkwardness) that stamps Grace, Tess and Arabella. They remain either cerebral: 'I like new sensations, I am curious, most things are so flat and boring.' (Iota (Kathleen Mannington Caffyn), *A Yellow Aster*, 1894, vol.2, p.51.) Or vaguely allusive: 'Touches and caresses and things of that sort bring thrills and shakes and trembles and flushes . . . . Well, I must practise touches and such, and hope for results; also, I must not let myself shiver and feel sick when I in my turn get them bestowed upon me.' (*Ibid.* vol.2, p.188.)

Hardy was disingenuous in the extreme when in writing his 1912 Postscript to the novel he spoke of having been 'informed' by others that Sue Bridehead seemed to be 'the woman of the feminist movement . . . who does not recognize the necessity for most of her sex to follow marriage as a profession' (*Jude the Obscure*, p.30). He was very familiar with New Woman fiction itself and with some of its writers, as his letters show: he privately endorsed for Mona Caird (author of *The Daughters of Danaus*, 1894) an essay on 'Evolution in Marriage' which never reached print; he congratulated 'George Egerton' (Mary Chavelita Clairmonte) on her *Keynotes*, first published 1893 (*Letters*, vol.2, p.102) with its radically subjective presentation of women as typically possessed of an 'untamed primitive savage temperament' (Reprint, 1983, p.22). And he expressed envy of 'Sarah Grand' (Frances Elizabeth MacFall), author of *The Heavenly Twins* (1893), who having offended her friends already can now 'write boldly, and get listened to' (*Letters*, vol.2, p.33).

Sue is marked out from the other women in Hardy's novels, and immediately identifiable as a New Woman, by her explicit awareness of herself as a member of an oppressed sex rightly seeking autonomy. In this she equates with Jude, the last representative of the poor man and the artist; hence the bond between them. As the multiple and contradictory critical interpretations of her serve to illustrate, her existence in the novel is a series of points at which different readings intersect, a 'series of seemings', such as the 1895 Preface recognises (*Jude the Obscure*, p.27). In crude terms she conforms to the hostile reading of the New Woman as a stereotype of demands, but some of these are of a new down-to-earth kind. She is first seen by Jude at work as a paid employee in a shop, a job she has chosen in preference to the conventionally genteel ones of teacher or governess. Her views on sex and marriage involve the right to marry a man she does not love and to leave him when she finds him physically repugnant. She can be seen as making large claims for herself and forcing them on others, particularly Phillotson, in a priggish fashion: 'J. S. Mill's words, those are. I have been reading it up. Why can't you act upon them? I wish to, always.' (*Ibid.* p.239.)

In contrast with other New Women she is, moreover, as unabashed as Grace in talking about her sexual life. She volunteers to Jude: 'I have never yielded myself to any lover . . . I have remained as I began . . . . Better women would not. People say I must be cold-natured – sexless – on account of it. But I won't have it! Some of the most passionately erotic poets have been the most self-contained in their daily lives.' (*Ibid.* pp.168–9.) She explicitly describes her attitude to her physical relationship with Phillotson: 'What tortures me so much is the necessity of being responsive to this man whenever he wishes . . . the dreadful contract to feel in a particular way in a matter whose essence is its voluntariness!' (*Ibid.* p.230.) She is prepared to elaborate at least four different reasons for her apparent frigidity towards Jude himself:

> Put it down to my timidity . . . to a woman's natural timidity when the crisis comes . . . But partly, perhaps, because it is by his generosity that I am now free, I would rather not be other than a little rigid . . . But don't press me . . . Assume that I haven't the courage of my opinions . . . My nature is not so passionate as yours! (*Ibid.* p.255.)

Where she differs from the crude stereotype is in seeing her 'rights' in terms of existential choices. Her uncertainty about her motives for refusing Jude physically is not seen by her as entailing uncertainty as to her right to say no whatever the reason. She is clear that: 'The social moulds civilization fits us into have no more relation to our actual shapes than the conventional shapes of the constellations have to the real star-patterns' (*ibid.* pp.222–3). She discards the conventional identification and labels, preferring her own existence: 'I am called Mrs Richard Phillotson, living a calm wedded life with my counterpart of that name. But I am not really Mrs Richard Phillotson, but a woman tossed about, all alone, with aberrant passions, and unaccountable antipathies.' (*Ibid.* p.222.) She presents to Jude, assuming his acceptance, a paradoxical demand for 'her right to a non-sexual love and her right to a non-marital sexual liaison' (Boumelha, 1982, p.143). Both Jude and the narrator faced with this new element in language have difficulty in construing her. Jude at least has not entirely lost his sense of the old significations of woman. At one time this surfaces as a sense that since male desire is paramount, forced union, as in Victorian marriage, is licit; at another time he sees her fleetingly as a fallen woman whom he has seduced: 'I seduced you . . . You were a distinct type – a refined creature, intended by Nature to be left intact. But I couldn't leave you alone!' (*Jude the Obscure*, p.352.)

The narrator, usually seeing things through Jude's eyes, is necessarily in the same difficulty as he. At times he seems to glimpse her autonomy, 'the elusiveness of her curious double-nature'. He even condemns her attempted adherence to the old womanly norms of marital loyalty in words that are 'so strictly proper and so lifelessly spoken that they might have been taken from a list of model speeches in "*The Wife's Guide to Conduct*" ' (*ibid.* p.206). Despite these liberal views, he obsessively returns to the essentialist view of women when he sees Sue as lacking logic (*ibid.* p.235), acting on the 'narrow womanly humours' of impulse (*ibid.* p.186), appropriately taking a womanly domestic role in her semi-detached relationship with Jude, having a woman's 'disregard of her dignity' when alone (*ibid.* p.279) and like other women ignorant of how men would wear out her heart and life (*ibid.* p.193). The old reading is recurrently magnetic for the narrator in spite of the many projections of an alternative, because his essentialism has a biological content. This is evident in the description of the seventy girls in the training school dormitory:

> they all lay in their cubicles, their tender feminine faces up-
> turned to the flaring gas-jets which at intervals stretched down
> the long dormitories, every face bearing the legend 'The Weaker'
> upon it, as the penalty of the sex wherein they were moulded, which

by no possible exertion of their willing hearts and abilities could be made strong while the inexorable laws of nature remain what they are. They formed a pretty, suggestive, pathetic sight, of whose pathos and beauty they were themselves unconscious, and would not discover till, amid the storms and strains of after-years, with their injustice, loneliness, child-bearing, and bereavement, their minds would revert to this experience as to something which had been allowed to slip past them insufficiently regarded. (*Ibid*. pp.160–1.)

These fluctuations are an example of what Catherine Belsey (Newton and Rosenfelt, 1985, p.51) calls 'subjectivity . . . in process', in a text which because of its contradictions and ambiguities interrogates traditional images of women by allowing new readings of them to conflict with the old. Blatantly the individual subject is not an entity, as the kaleidoscope of critical Sue (mis)construing indicates, and in this 'lies the possibility of change' in the subject created by language. In Hardy's language at least the rigid signification of *woman/womanly* has disappeared, leaving a fruitful ambiguity.

CHAPTER SIX

Narrative Syntax in the Later Novels

Underlying *The Woodlanders* and *Tess* are the familiar structures that underlie the earlier novels. But the previously tentative interrogation of their conventional assumptions here becomes forthright; and the narrator now subsumes this discourse, hostile to patriarchy, into his commentary. This new distancing from the old misogynistic generalisations is evident for instance, in the recantation of the reductive assertion in *Desperate Remedies* that for a woman 'her dress is part of her body' (p.155). The narrator articulates a new credo in relation to Grace Melbury: 'there can be hardly anything less connected with a woman's personality than drapery which she has neither designed, manufactured, cut, sewed, nor even seen, except by a glance of approval . . . The woman herself was a conjectural creature who had little to do with the outlines presented to Sherton eyes . . .' This is pushed further, to a point that questions the generic notion of 'woman'. The individual woman's 'true quality' can only be 'approximated', and that by careful analysis, 'by putting together a movement now and a glance then, in that patient attention which nothing but watchful loving-kindness ever troubles itself to give' (*The Woodlanders*, p.40).

The displacement of earlier clichés about women helps to inscribe a reader different from the long-standing, blushable 'Young Person' attacked by Hardy and others. Indeed, writing on *Jude* in 1896 Havelock Ellis suggests that a new young person can be inscribed jointly with the supposed 'adult' reader.

I must confess that to me it seems the merest cant to say that a
book has been written only to be read by elderly persons. In France,
where a different tradition has been established, the statement may
pass, but not in England nor in America, where the Young Person
has a firm grip of the novel, which she is not likely to lose . . . We
may take it that a novel . . . is open to all readers. (Cox, 1970,
p.312.)

Given this greater freedom, the narrators' accounts are complicated
only by that incomplete comprehension of the opposite sex shared
by all males in the late novels and sketched in Chapter 5. The explicit
defence of women in the narratorial commentaries is enhanced by
Hardy's now distinct transformations of narrative patterns. With the
choice of a husband in *The Woodlanders* and the fallen woman who
atones in *Tess* he negates the conventional implications of such plots.
Even with the newly developed variant of the 1880s in which
a woman seeks her fulfilment by rejecting marriage he alters a
discontinuity in syntax by eradicating sequences that tended in other
New Woman fiction elsewhere to re-emerge from the earlier tainted
patterns.

   Although all three novels were attacked for their immoral
plots, the grounds for outrage were usually *ad hoc*. However,
at least one critic recognised these transformations of narrative
syntax as striking at the foundations of the old novelistic language.
In the *National Review* for May 1896, A. J. Butler writing on
'Mr Hardy as a Decadent' said on the subject of 'renunciation'
in *The Woodlanders*:

   to every axiom, to every formula, come periods when its authority
   in some field or other ceases to be taken universaly for granted;
   and just now one of those periods seems to have set in with
   regard to those above mentioned. So far as they deal with the
   relations of men and women to each other the axiom is questioned,
   the formula is denied, and the 'problem' results. (*Ibid.* pp.287–8.)

Such a clamour for the old assertive and unquestioning kind of text
makes clear that this novel was, like *Tess* and *Jude* later, seen
as radically subversive of the linguistic system and so of society
itself. Thus Hardy is rebuked by Butler:

   When a man possessing Mr. Hardy's power of observation and
   knowledge of human nature, conscious as he must be that upon the
   validity of the axiom, the authority of the formula, the whole fabric

of society depends, when such a man gets caught by the fashion of the period, he turns upon society as if it were the creator of axiom and formula, instead of, in a sense, their creature, and rates it. (*Ibid*. p.288.)

Language, as Butler sees, is a public semiotic and ought to speak the man, not *vice versa*. Butler's comment is obliquely revealing in its reference to 'the fashion of the period', which captures the historical dimension of language and its ceaseless evolution: others besides Hardy were evidently involved in the process of upsetting the linguistic apple-cart. More strikingly his assessment of what Hardy is up to is accurate: 'the axiom is questioned, the formula is denied', not only in relation to womanly renunciation but to all that it stands for as well. What I wish to show is how this statement applies in turn to the plots of *The Woodlanders*, *Tess* and *Jude* in two respects: in their questioning of the traditional implications both of marriage stories and those of other sequences in which fallen women are falsely presented as agents. The details differ for each novel.

The writers represented by Butler's reference to 'the fashion of the period' had already in the late 1880s and early 1890s directed an attack on the fictional use of marriage as the closure of a linear sequence of events, representing 'the reinstatement of order' (Belsey, 1980, p.75) and an assurance of continuing stability. As I have shown in Chapter 5 the institution itself had begun to change, but only in ways that left its essential nature intact. However, the discussion that legal changes involved was accompanied by intense fictional scrutiny that continued for many years. Hardy in his later public contributions to debate was, as always, self-contradictory and inscrutable. In 1912 he wrote in *Nash's Magazine* that existing marriage laws were 'the gratuitous cause of at least half the misery of the community' (Orel, 1967, p.252). A month later in the 1912 Postscript to *Jude* he affects surprise at being charged with responsibility for the ' "shop-soiled" condition of the marriage theme' (*Jude the Obscure*, p.29).

But privately he expressed views which substantiate Butler's description of him as a revolutionary. In a letter of November 1906 to Millicent Fawcett, the suffragette, he speaks of his approval of women getting the vote because he feels this will lead to the breaking up of 'the present pernicious conventions in respect of manners, customs, religion, illegitimacy, the stereotyped household (that it must be the unit of society), the father of a woman's child (that it is anybody's business but the woman's own . . .)' (*Letters*, vol.3, p.238). He makes the same point in a letter to Helen Ward, in December 1908, about the likely break-up of 'the present marriage-system, the present social rules of other sorts, religious codes, legal arrangements on property, &c . . .' (*ibid.* p.360). This, he says, he does not consider 'a bad thing' or he would not have written *Jude*. These private opinions show a clear understanding of the widespread ramifications of the institution that he wished to see overthrown. It is a picture of a desired state of affairs diametrically opposed to that in fictional narratives, where series of events leading to a marriage are articulated as development towards a state of stability. In all three novels this picture of stability is deleted by the over-writing of alternative accounts of marriage disintegrating. The chief syntactic feature of these accounts is a recursiveness of plot that figures an opposition to stability and order.

An over-writing of traditional plots also questions their usual implications that in choosing husbands or making atonement for a sexual fall women are in a strong sense agents; agency is even seen as ultimately lacking in the new pattern where women refuse marriage. In *The Woodlanders* Grace (like Fancy Day earlier) chooses a husband. But the event is displaced from the usual final position to part way through the narrative. At the same time it is decentred: for though there is discussion about it, the ceremony is erased from the text and is already a past event when referred to in the last sentence of chapter twenty-four: 'Five hours later she was the wife of Fitzpiers.' (*The Woodlanders*, p.164.) By the opening of the next chaper the honeymoon is over and Grace as a married woman is seen, significantly, alone. This apparent erasure of Fitzpiers in the role of husband continues, since the marriage takes the form mainly of a series of absences on his part, culminating in his final elopement and departure with Felice Charmond.

This unemphatic analysis of the marriage and its breakdown is accompanied by an account of the development of Grace's feelings in which the method is to delete the traditional by superimposing another view. The two views are visible, one below the other, in the description of her emotions before the ceremony. Uppermost is 'a certain anticipative satisfaction, the satisfaction of feeling that she would be the heroine of an hour; moreover she was proud, as a cultivated woman, to be the wife of a cultivated man' (*ibid*. p.163). Below this is discernible what she does not feel, but what conventionally she would be expected to feel:

> But what an attenuation this cold pride was of the dream of her youth, in which she had pictured herself walking in state towards the altar flushed by the purple light and bloom of her own passion, without a single misgiving as to the sealing of the bond, and fervently receiving as her due 'the homage of a thousand hearts; the fond deep love of one'. (*Ibid*. pp.163–4.)

Even her moderate pride and satisfaction are similarly cancelled by later over-writing, describing the perceived shame of her return to the adulterous Fitzpiers. This event too is marginalised by occurring haphazardly as the result of a chance encounter with the man-trap that throws her into his arms. Their reunion is effected, like most events in the marriage, by a narrative absence. This time it is a joint one as the two go off to Fitzpiers' lodging at the Earl of Wessex, instead of Grace returning to her father's house. The shamefulness of this erases even her original modest sense of achievement, when her father finds her finally at the inn, looking as 'if she lived there, but in other respects rather guilty and frightened.' The banality of what she has done is stressed by their exchange at such a pivotal moment:

> 'I thought you went out to get parsley!'
> 'O yes – I did – but it is all right . . . I am here with Edred. It is entirely owing to an accident, father.'
> 'Edred – an accident? . . . I thought he was two hundred mile off!'
> 'Yes – so he is – I mean, he has got a beautiful practice two hundred miles off – he has bought it with his own money . . . But he travelled here, and I was nearly caught in a man-trap, and that's how it is I am here.' (*Ibid*. p.334.)

Added to this over-writing is the recursive treatment of the Fitzpiers' marriage. This diminished second union is not itself stable but the beginning of a cycle of infidelities that will recur endlessly, presumably followed by endless reunions. As Hardy put it in a letter, catching the sense of diminishing returns: 'the reunited husband and wife are supposed to live ever after unhappily – or at any rate not quite happily' (*Letters*, vol.1, p.196). In the text itself the law of recursiveness is stated by Melbury (in a textually recursive process of embedding). In 1887 was added, to his final speech: 'Well – he's her husband . . . but it's a forlorn hope for her; and God knows how it will end!' In 1895 this was changed, after 'husband', to:

> . . . and let her take him back to her bed if she will! . . . But let her bear in mind that the woman walks and laughs somewhere at this very moment whose neck he'll be colling next year as he does hers to-night; and as he did Felice Charmond's last year; and Suke Damson's the year afore! . . . It's a forlorn hope for her . . . [etc.] (*The Woodlanders*, p.335 and p.46 of Introduction.)

The recurrence of infidelity and compromise mimics the instability of the legal institution, in contradiction of the conventional fictional use. Along with this demonstration of the spuriousness of marriage as closure the novel also exhibits the meretriciousness of the implication in the pattern when a woman chooses a husband that she is a free agent. Superficially Grace chooses Fitzpiers as a husband and rechooses him after Giles' death. But in both instances the lack of space in which she may exert her free will is evident: his role as her husband is overdetermined by her education, by social pressure, by the instilled sense of duty and by Fitzpiers' experience and manipulativeness. From the start she expresses in her person 'a tendency to wait for others' thoughts before uttering her own: possibly also to wait for others' deeds before her own doings' (*ibid*. p.40). Her upbringing allows her father to take a crudely pre-emptive line over Fitzpiers' approaches:

> 'I needn't tell you to make it all smooth for him.'
> 'You mean, to lead him on to marry me?'
> 'I do. Haven't I educated you for it?' (*Ibid*. p.149.)

This, combining with Fitzpiers' physical attractiveness ('the strange influence he exercised upon her whenever he came near her') leaves her 'in an excitement which was not love, not

ambition; rather a fearful consciousness of hazard in the air . . .'
(*ibid*. p.153). She agrees to an engagement, recognising him not
only as in many senses 'irresistible' but also as 'coercive' (*ibid*.
p.155). The second 'choosing' of Fitzpiers is similarly charted
as predetermined: external pressures (matched from within) lead
her back to him. As in the original match social pressure is
exerted by her father after Giles' death (*ibid*. p.301), and
flattery and social enticements through Fitzpiers. The internal
pressure to conformity is evidenced by her re-reading of the
marriage service and her recognition of the 'awfully solemn
promises' she made when marrying him (*ibid*. p.327).

True, in the central section of the narrative there is a temporary
shift to agency on Grace's part. Before Felice's confession that
she is Fitzpiers' mistress and before their elopement, the narrator
has observed with approval the resurgence of her romantic
feelings for Giles. In her thoughts at least she is partly free:
'Nature was bountiful . . . No sooner had she been cast aside
by Edred Fitzpiers than another being, impersonating chivalrous
and undiluted manliness, had arisen out of the earth, ready to
her hand.' (*Ibid*. p.193.) But the celebration of this growing
autonomy and freedom to choose, described in Chapter 5, is
brief. They remain velleities; external circumstances are allowed
to press in and prevent their becoming substantial. She cannot
act out her own newly discovered meaning. She is timid until
too late in encouraging Giles, deterred, despite her bold remarks
about her lack of moral obligation to an unfaithful husband, by
the discovery that divorce is not possible. She cannot give
physical reality to her claim; she goes no further than a verbal
assertion that she is Giles' mistress, even under the extreme
pressure of pursuit by Fitzpiers. Her lack of will helps ensure
Giles' death; and she seems best satisfied by the ritualistic and
pointless servicing of Giles' grave, a morally hygienic act which,
particularly when Marty chaperons it, commits her to nothing.
She ignores Fitzpiers' (presumably devious) offer to make
divorce technically possible, if that is what she wishes, by going
away 'for ever' (*ibid*. p.316). Thus, in this supposedly calm,
autumnal work Hardy boldly unstabilises the traditional marriage
story exposing the lack of agency it involved for a woman and
revealing undeniably her object status.

In *Tess* the belated subtitle 'A Pure Woman' is itself already a direction to read the text as an over-writing of the traditional fallen-woman-atones stories. I now wish to examine such a reading and also to show the underlying lack of agency involved. In fact the subtitle accepts in advance some of the conventional assumptions that usually underlie such a narrative. Generic 'woman' is up for moral assessment and it is in respect of sexual morality that it is felt appropriate, even essential, to assess her: is she pure or not pure? To that extent the text colludes with the familiar pattern. What is destabilised, however, is the account of what it means for a woman to be sexually pure or blameless.

Characteristically Havelock Ellis grasped the problem that faced Hardy here and wrote of *Tess*:

> I was repelled at the outset by the sub-title . . . I have always regarded the conception of *purity*, when used in moral discussions, as a conception sadly in need of analysis, and almost the first time I ever saw myself in print was as the author of a discussion . . . of the question: 'What is Purity?' . . . It seems to me doubtful whether anyone is entitled to use the word 'pure' without first defining precisely what he means, and still more doubtful whether an artist is called upon to define it at all, even in several hundred pages. I can quite conceive that the artist should take pleasure in the fact that his own creative revelation of life poured contempt on many old prejudices. But such an effect is neither powerful nor legitimate unless it is engrained in the texture of the narrative; it cannot be stuck on by a label. (Cox, 1970, p.305.)

What Ellis seems to be saying more subtly than Butler, and with approval not disapproval, is that the artist *should* question the axiom and deny the formula. He does not realise that his unease with the subtitle suggests that *Tess* does precisely this: it destabilises the notion of 'purity' in a way that undermines that subtitle.

It is important not to assume that Tess is pure merely because she is not the victim of outright rape by Alec. This is made clearer by Hardy's progressive alterations of the text. Though he added in 1891 a description of Alec as 'the spoiler' (*Tess of the D'Urbervilles*, p.102), and one to Tess' being overheard sobbing on the night of the scene in the chase (*ibid*. p.127), other revisions render the scene more ambiguous by suggesting co-operation on her part. For instance, in 1892, he removed the reference to Alec as 'the spoiler' and to his drugging Tess with cordial or (earlier) spirits (*ibid*. p.100) which had been in the text from the manuscript stage. After her escape from Trantbridge Alec says to her in an early version: 'You didn't come for love of me . . .' She replies: ' 'Tis quite true . . . If I had ever really loved you, if I loved you still, I should not so loathe and hate myself for my weakness as I do now!' In 1892 'really' was changed to 'sincerely' and Tess concluded: 'My eyes were dazed by you for a little, and that was all.' (*Ibid*. p.109.) Similarly in 1891 to a description of her thoughts when confessing to her mother was added:

> She had dreaded him, winced before him, succumbed to . . . advantages he took of her helplessness; then, temporarily blinded by his flash manners, had been stirred to confused surrender awhile: had suddenly despised and disliked him, and had run away. (*Ibid*. p.117.)

Even this was taken a step further by the replacement in 1912 of 'flash' by 'ardent'. As others have pointed out the rape–seduction scene is followed by 'some few weeks' in which Tess remains Alec's mistress (*ibid*. p.107). She describes herself as 'mastered' (*ibid*. p.111) by him, with implications not only of force.

The breaking down of the line between rape and seduction, already mentioned earlier, is only one aspect of this sequence in the narrative. Another is that Tess has been physically drawn to Alec in a way retrospectively described as 'natural'. There develops a subtext about Tess, sexuality and naturalness that urges the exclusion of purely sexual relationships from the sphere of moral judgement. By implication Tess in a less artificial world might have regarded such a relationship as an available option. This is paradoxical: it cannot be logically reconciled with the equally urgent assertion that she is the victim of exploitation. But it seems to be the main ground for regarding her as pure, and alludes to some contemporary accounts of naturalness such as one of several produced by 'George Egerton' that Hardy copied out in January 1894: 'Men manufactured an artificial morality, made sins of things that were as clean in themselves as the pairing of . . . birds on the wing; crushed nature, robbed it of its beauty & meaning, & established a system that means war . . . because it is a struggle between instinctive truths and cultivated lies.' (Björk, 1985, vol.2, p.61.) Purity ultimately, as Ellis saw, escapes definition in *Tess*, except through the negation of old prejudices that would equate it with virginity and ignorance.

What is also innovatory in the syntax of *Tess* is that her punitive death is not the direct consequence of her fall: she survives her child's death, Angel's desertion and Alec's reappearance. Between the fall that is not a fall and her death is inserted a new sequence in which, like Elfride Swancourt, she lives through a period of autonomy before she dies. But whereas Elfride's marriage to Luxellian and innocent death in childbirth are tangential to the narrative, Tess's acts of will represent the culmination of the whole sequence. The events involved figure the monstrousness of the only choice that is left to her, the only meaning she can express after the final shock of Angel's coming to claim her when she has already returned to Alec as his mistress. In stabbing Alec to release herself for Angel she feels free even from guilt. As the latter listens to her confession of murder 'his horror at her impulse was mixed with amazement at the strength of her affection for himself; and at the strangeness of its quality, which had apparently extinguished her moral sense altogether' (*Tess of the D'Urbervilles*, p.524).

But Tess has formulated Alec's death to herself as logical, just as the truly autonomous Ethelberta formulated her marriage to Mountclere in that way: 'I thought as I ran along that you would be sure to forgive me now I have done that. It came to me as a shining light that I should get you back that way . . . I was unable to bear your not loving me. Say you do now, dear dear husband . . . now I have killed him!' (*Ibid.* pp.523–4.) Her logic is mad, but for once she dominates him:

> It was very terrible, if true: if a temporary hallucination, sad. But anyhow here was this deserted wife of his, this passionately fond woman, clinging to him without a suspicion that he would be anything to her but a protector. He saw that for him to be otherwise was not, in her mind, within the region of the possible. (*Ibid.* p.525.)

And he submits to her account of the possible.

There is no doubt that in her refusal to escape she still leads Angel, although she is clear as to the consequences of her act. It is she who, ironically, suggests that after her death he should marry her sister, Liza-Lu, realising that this would constitute legal incest: 'People marry sister-laws continually about Marlott.' (*Ibid.* p.536.) When she stretches out on the oblong slab at Stonehenge she is choosing her place of surrender. The death on the gallows that supervenes reveals the hollowness of her autonomy, a pretence with which Angel has colluded, knowing that they were out of time. Significantly she now says to him, with an understanding that goes beyond madness: 'I have had enough; and now I shall not live for you to despise me' (*ibid.* p.539). Like all fallen women she dies; all she has really been able to choose is the particular form of her death. Murder and execution as the only available expression of autonomy speak for themselves as to the real limits of agency for a fallen woman. Plot, as so often in Hardy, figures a central statement.

Jude, unlike *The Woodlanders* and *Tess*, has as its narrative matrix a pattern of recent origin: a woman rejecting marriage. Like theirs, however, its narrative syntax is innovatory in its transformation of the pattern. But attached also to this central nexus are many nodes, which since they involve spectacularly recurrent marriages repeat the destabilising of the institution found in *The Woodlanders*. Thus, Jude marries Arabella twice; Sue twice marries Phillotson; Arabella contracts two more marriages, one bigamous, one legal; and she projects a fifth to Vilbert after Jude's death. Recursiveness becomes frenetic, figuring marriage through plot as a farcical game that is the antithesis of stability. The effect of farce was noticed (scathingly) by several contemporary reviewers, one of whom spoke of how 'The crowning absurdity of the double re-marriage makes the whole book appear dangerously near to farce.' (Cox, 1970, p.251.)

But the matrix narrative sequence in *Jude* is that taken from the New Women novels in which Sue, after leaving her husband Phillotson, claims the right to live unmarried with Jude (though, to his surprise, she also claims the right to remain sexually uncommitted). The New Women in the novels of the 1890s, which were given that label, are usually perceived as individuals attempting to rewrite themselves by claiming the agency so long thought to have been denied them in fiction. Since marriage has been presented as the only option, their self-assertion takes the form of rejecting it either before or after the ceremony. The potential significance of such rejection was huge, and one or two women writers grasped this. George Egerton's heroine in 'Virgin Soil' when discussing the manipulativeness of wives articulates a radically subversive view of woman's traditional lot:

> I don't blame them; it must be so, as long as marriage is based on such unequal terms, as long as man demands from a wife as a right, what he must sue from a mistress as a favour; until marriage becomes for many women a legal prostitution, a nightly degradation, a hateful yoke under which they age, mere bearers of children conceived in a sense of duty, not love. They bear them, birth them, nurse them, and begin again without choice in the matter, growing old, unlovely . . . until their love, granted they started with that . . . is turned into a duty they submit to with distaste instead of a favour granted to a husband who must become a new lover to obtain it. (Egerton, 1983, p.155.)

Gail Cunningham in *The New Woman and the Victorian Novel* sees the exponents of this new pattern as texts in which all the women concerned act initially on high-minded principles such as Egerton's Florence enunciates (Cunningham, 1978). This is a reductive account: some act on principle, others pragmatically. With those who take a principled stand, it is sometimes on one principle, sometimes another. All escapes or attempts to escape into unmapped territory are necessarily erratic; where there is no established route, self-assertion will be idiosyncratic. This is clear if the familiar examples of new women rejecting marriage are examined.

There are those who reject it after the ceremony. Among these Evadne Frayling in Sarah Grand's *The Heavenly Twins* (1893) 'declines to live with' her husband, now revealed as a debauchee. Her grounds are partly practical, since he may pass on venereal disease, and partly theoretical since she wishes not to be seen as 'countenancing vice' (Grand, 1893, vol.1, p.98): 'I would strip the imposition, approved of custom, connived at by parents, made possible by the state of ignorance in which we are carefully kept – the imposition upon a young girl's innocence and inexperience of a disreputable man for a husband' (*ibid.* p.97). Somewhat inconsistently, she eventually agrees to live with him, though without consummating the marriage. On the other hand, the husband that Gwen Waring rejects in *A Yellow Aster* (Iota, 1894) is a reputable man whom she has married without love as an experiment. It is pregnancy that opens her eyes to a sense that she is involved in what Egerton calls 'legal prostitution': her condition, she feels, 'is degradation, feeling towards him as I do, and as I've always done! . . . Talk of the shame of women who have children out of the pale of marriage, it's nothing to the shame of those who have children and don't love.' (*Ibid.* pp.79–81.) What she does is separate from her husband while keeping up a social pretence. A third wife who takes a stand after marriage is Hadria Fullerton in Mona Caird's *The Daughters of Danaus* (Caird, 1894). She has neither Evadne's experience nor Gwen's; she marries a blameless husband and has several children before a very general sense that marriage is an intolerable oppression overcomes what she calls a 'sickly feminine conscience' (*ibid.* p.194). Distinctively, though a mother, she sees that 'children had been the unfailing means of bringing women into line with tradition' (*ibid.* p.187). She rejects women's 'frenzied sense of duty' as 'stupid and degrading' (*ibid.* p.207). She acts vigorously by removing herself to Paris to study music. These three women demonstrate the lack of uniformity that prevails in their perceived motives and in their actions.

The same is true of New Women, who reject marriage before the event, not after. The most obviously principled rejection is that of the heroine of a text by a male author: Herminia Barton in Grant Allen's notorious best-seller *The Woman Who Did* (Allen, 1895). She is faced neither by a debauchee nor a man that she does not love; on the contrary she is passionately attracted to the man who proposes to her, Alan Merrick. Her reaction is outrage, on two grounds: that, like the narrator, she hates 'monopolist' physical instincts (*ibid.* p.184); and that marriage is, as a consequence, degrading. And she sees the proposal of marriage as a lack of understanding: 'Don't tell me,

after all I've tried to make you feel and understand, you thought
I could possibly consent to *marry* you! . . . Would you have me
like the blind girls who go unknowing to the altar, as sheep go
to the shambles?' (*Ibid*. pp.35–6.) Having converted him to her
radical view, she carries out her intention by living as his wife,
unmarried. Other supposed stands against marriage are less
extreme. Jessamine Halliday in Emma Frances Brooke's *A
Superfluous Woman* (1894) only prefers a sexual liaison to
marriage because Colin Macgillvray is a Scottish crofter whose
social class rules him out as a good match. Her attempt to
rewrite herself is evident only in the lengthy struggles with the
physical attraction she feels towards Macgillvray and her
unwomanly attempt to seduce him. In the event when this fails
she opts for 'the best match' in Europe, the syphilitic Lord
Heriot. Similarly, the eponymous heroine of Ménie Muriel
Dowie's *Gallia* (Dowie, 1895) is an ambivalent rebel. She does
not reject marriage entirely but by deciding only to take it on
her own terms: since the man she loves, Dark Essex, rejects
her, she decides to choose a partner on eugenic grounds and
marry without love 'solely with a view to the child I am going
to live for' (*ibid*. p.218).

Rejection of marriage in these texts is demonstrably not offered
in homogeneous sequences. And into the spectrum of eccentric
attempts to break out of the traditional womanly norms of
behaviour the 'obscure' Sue Bridehead, with her paradoxical
double claim about her relationships with men, fits as one more
anomaly.

What also happens to most of these texts syntactically is
something else that Cunningham fails to recognise: that when
the women find and accept a suitable husband or atone for sexual
error by death, agency is, as usual, withdrawn from them, with
the collusion of the narrator. Her account is that the novels
conform to a regular new 'common pattern' which shows 'the
heroine arriving at her ideals of freedom and equality from
observation of her society, but then being brought through the
miserable experience of trying to put them into practice to a
position of weary disillusion' (Cunningham, 1978, p.50). This
sounds like a perfectly articulated syntactic structure. In practice
this is not so. The 'ideals' to which the resolution of the pattern

is assumed to refer back are, as I have shown, bizarrely personal; the assertion that the remainder of the narrative coheres is not well-founded. The existing structures that embody prevailing ideologies exert a powerful counter influence to produce broken-backed structures. Only one or two writers like Mona Caird and Hardy began to produce the new syntactic pattern that Cunningham postulates for all.

So Evadne, Gwen and Gallia all eventually submit to a husband in sequences which are underwritten by the narrator as is Fancy Day's marriage to Dick Dewy. Evadne's submissiveness to her male mentor, Dr Galbraith, is treated with a Trollopian playfulness. He, now narrating, speaks of his surprise at her reacting to his proposal of marriage by going off in a 'ridiculous tantrum simply because I did not begin by expressing my love for her' (Grand, 1893, p.244). It is a familiar example of the male cat-and-mouse technique which ends with her clinging to him physically and psychologically. Gwen Waring, in an atmosphere thick with sentimentality, returns to the husband she wrongly believes dead and croons to her baby an *ad hoc* recantation of her former unwomanliness: ' . . . your mother had the best man that God yet made or will make, to love her . . . Baby, she killed this man who loved her . . . because she was unnatural and couldn't love' (Iota, 1894, pp. 200–1). Gallia, after coolly choosing a repentant roué as a father for her intended child, flutters with pretty rebellion at finding herself caught in a 'net of sentiment'. But she happily agrees to take 'Queen Nature's shilling' in the form of a posy of honeysuckle and meadowsweet (Dowie, 1895, p.314). Her continued verbal protests are subsumed into an archly disbelieving narratorial commentary that turns 'no' into 'yes' (*ibid.* p.315). When Mark Gurdon kisses her the narrator remarks that 'Being only a simple young woman after all, this had a great effect upon her. If only Essex had had the grit to go as far – to laugh and go as far' (*ibid.* p.326). The final revelation that Essex is restrained by hereditary heart disease completes the sense that the healthy and repentant Gurdon is the right husband after all.

On the other hand, Jessamine, who has before marriage indulged in passionate sexual desires and even attempted to seduce Macgillvray, meets the typical fate of a fallen woman:

madness and death. True, she is being punished for her wicked marriage as well as her pre-marital adventures but her protracted illness and death are the manifestation of a guilt that is assumed to be well-motivated. The coincidence of conventional sexual fall and death is also found even in the resolutely libertarian Herminia. Having lived according to her principles as an unmarried mother, she commits suicide, since it is the only means left to repair the social and emotional injury she has done to her conventionally-minded daughter. Her suicide note says to the girl: 'Accept this reparation. For all the wrong I may have done, all the mistakes I may have made, I sincerely and earnestly implore your forgiveness' (Allen, 1895, p.238). As with Tess her range of choices is narrowed to one fatal option. In neither of these works does the narratorial commentary offset the compromise figured by events.

What both these types of New Woman show is the re-emergence of the long-dominant and tainted patterns discussed in the first part of this chaper and in Chapter 3. As with the shift in the meaning of ideologically determined signs, the shift to new patterns of syntax is a slow process. The patterns concealing women's lack of agency refuse to be deleted and overwritten: they re-emerge in the latter half of most of the novels under discussion to produce broken-backed structures, hybrid sequences, syntactic anacolutha. However, some few examples which bridge this discontinuity in syntax can be found, and *Jude* is among them (as is Caird's *The Daughters of Danaus*).

The structure of plot in *Jude* conforms to the syntactical regularity that Cunningham speaks of. Sue's assertion of personal autonomy, described in Chapter 5, depends on her assumption that it overrides other claims, including the traditional ones of husband, children and society. It withers under the onslaught of an event that relates directly to her being a female, like the girls in the Training School dormitory. The extreme fact of her children's death is precipitated in part by her miscalculation when Father Time questions her about her pregnancy. Her over-sophisticated answer leads him to the conclusion that 'If we children was gone there'd be no trouble at all!' (*Jude the Obscure*, p.344.) Consequently she makes a link between her unconventionality and the deaths: she is manifestly a bad mother.

With the mad logic of a Tess she then links this with her sexuality which has resulted in the children's existence and that too is predicated as tainted. There is then an exterior and interior appropriateness in returning to Phillotson's bed: he is still her 'real' husband; and marital relations with him represent what she finds most repugnant and therefore most suitable as a punishment. The blending of this with a collapse into religiosity makes plain the parallel hold of institutionalised religion and institutionalised marriage.

The links back made by the narrator with the earlier sequences provide syntactically perfect articulation. He now recognises that the strongest aid to the outside social pressures which enforce the womanly ideal comes from within, and in particular from the maternal instinct. He contrasts the present with a time when 'her intellect scintillated like a star' (*ibid*. p.351). Loss of agency, cynically presented in *The Woodlanders* and *Tess*, is here mourned over by both Jude and the narrator and perceived by them as equivocal as to its source. Jude ponders an essentialist view, wondering whether a woman is 'a thinking unit at all' or merely 'a fraction always wanting its integer' (*ibid*. p.359). She has returned to old forms, forcing him back on generalisations that see women after all as intuitive not rational, inferior not equal. But this is a view now distanced from the narrator who regards Sue as not a real woman but the ghost of her former self and in fetters. The collapse of female autonomy is seen as inevitable and disastrous. This is a new perspective, not found in most New Woman novels; with this novel Hardy furthers the development of an innovatory narrative pattern as he furthered the development of the new alternative sign for woman.

CHAPTER SEVEN

The Well-Beloved as Metatext

The Well-Beloved is and is not Hardy's last novel. No manuscript exists but the serial version, *The Pursuit of the Well-Beloved, A Sketch of a Temperament* was printed in the *Illustrated London News* from 1 October to 17 December 1892 (hereafter *The Pursuit* always refers to this 1892 version). In book form there was published, in March 1897, *The Well-Beloved, A Sketch of a Temperament*, a text usually regarded as definitive and yet simultaneously as a variant of the 1892 version (hereafter *The Well-Beloved* always refers to the 1897 version). By this sleight-of-hand a date of 1892 is attributed to the work and *Jude the Obscure* (volume edition 1895) is somewhat confusedly assigned the status of the last novel that Hardy wrote. There are, however, pragmatic reasons for giving equal status to the texts of 1892 and 1897 (as well as theoretical ones that I have discussed elsewhere). Chief among these reasons are major differences in plot between the two: Pearston (the name for the central figure in 1892) in *The Pursuit* marries twice, once bigamously; Pierston (the name for the central figure in 1897) only once in *The Well-Beloved* as a belated act of kindness to an ageing former mistress. Pearston attempts seduction and suicide, Pierston neither. Such differences (and there are many others) are enough to distinguish the two works as discrete.

The central core shared (with individual variations) by the two texts is the story of a sculptor, Jocelyn Pearston/Pierston, who pursues throughout his life a migrating 'Well-Beloved' whom he finds embodied sequentially under many names: 'To his Well-

Beloved he had always been faithful; but she had had many embodiments. Each individuality known as Lucy, Jane, Flora, Evangeline, or whatnot, had been merely a transient condition of her.' (*The Well-Beloved*, p.34.) The physical approximations have varied too: 'She was a blonde, a brunette, tall, *petite*, *svelte*, straight-featured, full, curvilinear. Only one quality remained unalterable: her instability of tenure.' (*Ibid*. p.64.) In the main story-line she is incarnate under the name Avice Caro, borne by three generations of women in the same family: the first a romantic ingenue, the second a knowing coquette and the third a shy, well-educated and virginal creature. In the serial Pearston, at the age of 60, marries the unwilling third Avice, in the book version she elopes with a man of her own age on the eve of the wedding.

Interwoven with these affairs is the story of another temporary incarnation, Marcia Bencomb, an Arabella figure, whom he marries in *The Pursuit* but with whom he has only a brief liaison in *The Well-Beloved*. She re-enters his life in the final scenes of both works. Pearston's/Pierston's artistic life runs parallel to all this since his sculpture consists in endlessly trying to capture Aphrodite, the goddess of love, in stone from the Isle of Slingers (Portland) whence all these characters somewhat incestuously derive, as the reader is constantly reminded. I shall therefore treat *The Pursuit* and *The Well-Beloved* as a further development of that openness already developing in the endings of Victorian novels: as a double form with not merely alternative endings but alternative texts, an either/or structure. This syntactically co-ordinated branching is completely innovatory.

The Well-Beloved has always been regarded as in some way exceptional. The hostile critic in *The World* who saw it as an illustration of Hardy's 'sex-mania' still ironically recognised its uniqueness: 'It may be fairly admitted that in the whole range of fiction from the days of the Greek author of *The Wonders of Thule* down to Mr. Hardy himself, there is nothing at all approximating to the plot of *The Well-Beloved*.' (*The World*, 24 March 1897, p.13.) Hardy himself, at least in the Preface to the volume in the 1912 edition, thought so too, believing the story to differ 'from all or most others of the series in that the interest aimed at is of an ideal or subjective nature' (*The Well-Beloved*, p.26). The extreme contrivance of plot, a repetition suggestive at once of mathematical progression and of a fairy tale, draws attention to its own fictiveness. This struck that most self-referential of novelists, Proust, who makes Marcel describe the work as an outstanding example of the 'stonemason's geometry' that is the summation of Hardy's artistry (Proust, *The Captive*, Part 2, 1968, pp.235–6). Often its extraordinariness has been strikingly displayed by its absence from general critical studies of Hardy's fiction such as Ian Gregor's *The Great Web* (1974). It is not only a double text but often an absent one too.

It is perhaps, then, a recent interest in linguistic absence combining with an interest in self-referentiality that has reinstated it as a (conveniently empty) centre of the canon. Two explicit accounts of the reinstatement are John Fowles' 'Hardy and the Hag' (Butler, 1977, pp.28–42) and J. Hillis Miller's 'The Well-Beloved: The Compulsion to Stop Repeating' (*Fiction and Repetition*, 1982). Fowles sees the work as expressive of 'a nausea at the fictionality of fiction . . . or as a dread of once more entering an always ultimately defeating labyrinth' (Butler, *Thomas Hardy after 50 Years*, 1977, p.30). Hillis Miller develops the same idea of self-reference:

> As with many great writers, a central theme of Hardy's writing is literature itself, its nature and powers. More or less hidden in the earlier novels, this theme surfaces in . . . the form of an interrogation of the relation between erotic fascination, creativity, and Platonic metaphysics which makes *The Well-Beloved* one of a group of important nineteenth-century novels about art. (*Fiction and Repetition*, p.148.)

Certainly this text is self-referential, not only locally but in relation to the whole 'Great Web' that is Hardy's fiction. Many connections, transpositions or alternative working out of incidents between novels have become clear in earlier chapters. I have demonstrated elsewhere the inter-connectedness of Hardy's 'final trilogy' of 'provisional narratives', *The Pursuit, Jude* and *The Well-Beloved* (see Butler, *Alternative Hardy*, forthcoming Macmillan, 1989). Other critics have argued for links between texts or groups of texts. As I shall show, I regard *The Pursuit* and *The Well-Beloved*, taken together, as a metatext which reflects on all Hardy's preceding novels. Unlike Hillis Miller, I do not see the earlier novels as capable of summary under the heading of texts which pose the question

'Why is it that most human beings go through life somnambulistically, compelled to repeat the same mistakes in love, so inflicting on themselves and on others the same suffering, again and again?' (*Ibid.* p.150.)

I think that the 'covert structure and meaning of Hardy's earlier novels' which are in this novel 'brought more fully into the open' (*ibid.* p.151) is operative at a level on which feminine and masculine are *not* subsumed into the category of human beings (which seems in the end, like many such subsumings, to be masculine). On the contrary, as I have shown, they develop a dialectical structure as the appropriating voice of patriarchy falters before the women that Hardy creates. Thus, an alternative discourse alongside the original misogyny begins to emerge even in the early novels, and more fully from *The Woodlanders* onwards. What *The Well-Beloved* does is reflect upon this artistic process of attempt and resistance. And the alternative plots of the double text figure plainly that breakdown of the conventional power-hierarchy which fuels the dialectic. This is the historical and less than universal dimension that Hillis Miller overleaps.

One specificity that is overlooked is the crucial nature of the isolation of this particular artist-figure, so different from the social disvaluing his prototypes experience in the early novels. With Jocelyn the sympathetic bond of perceived social inferiority which bound together narrator and artist is no longer in place. He is viewed with a cold eye. For him class is an absence rather than a state of mind, a fact to which the narrator ironically draws attention. Early on the point is cynically made that 'the sculptor of budding fame' effortlessly condescends to receive from his father, 'an inartistic man of trade and commerce merely', a yearly allowance, 'pending the famous days to come' (*The Well-Beloved*, p.30).

The compromises of the artistic market place are also overtly in evidence in his friend and mentor Somers who, once married, devotes himself to the production of consumer goods, 'executing . . . many pleasing aspects of nature addressed to the furnishing householder through the middling critic' (*ibid.* p.157). By this means Somers affords a sumptuous style of living and the education of a family of daughters. Jocelyn (I shall use the Christian name when I do not wish to refer to one text rather than another) assumes himself to be quite different but the text throws this into question. When he wonders idly whether, like Somers, to play the 'jackal to this lion of a family and house and studio and social reputation' (*ibid*. p.158) he returns no answer. But his putative jackaldom raises the question of why already he has been so successful financially and 'prospered without effort', while believing himself to be indifferent to 'the popular reception of his dream-figures' (*ibid*. p.63). Such a belief begins to look like an example of his characteristic double-think in the light of the narrator's further gloss: 'these dreams he translated into plaster, and found that by them he was hitting a public taste he had never aimed at, and mostly despised' (*ibid*. p.64). Significantly it is Somers, the enthusiastic entrepreneur, who, to dissuade him from not attending an unheroic-sounding 'Academy night' dubs him 'our only inspired sculptor . . . our Praxiteles, or rather our Lysippus' (*ibid*. p.85). Since Praxiteles, a sculptor of Aphrodite figures, is a more appropriate analogy than Lysippus, a realist, Somers' artistic judgement is effectively undercut. The artist has become a dubious figure, possibly ungifted, probably venal, certainly comic, rather than a suitably ravaged representative of the human race.

I agree with Fowles and Hillis Miller, of course, that *The Well-Beloved* is a work about, not just involving, art, but the art that Jocelyn is engaged in is always and only the representation of women. The novel may have implications about art in general, but they must derive from what it has to say about women-focused art such as Jocelyn's statues of female nudes and Hardy's stories of women and womanliness (in which the latter correlates with the notion of the ideal Well-Beloved). The text, in its double form, reflects on what such art does with women: the nature and extent of its attempted appropriation of them which, it demonstrates, inevitably fails. The move to appropriate and the failure of the move is figured in Jocelyn's obsessive attempts to capture in stone a unitary 'essence' of Aphrodite. For all his public profit there is talk from him of failure in his task. His vaunted sculpture is perceived by the reader as so much dusty lumber when he lures the domesticated second Avice to his

London flat with the suggestion that it will give her the chance
'to dust all my Venus failures . . . and other objects' (*ibid*. p.119).
The appropriation of women, first attempted in *Desperate
Remedies* when the heroine is endowed with the astonishing
name, Cytherea, an Aphrodite variant, is now scrutinised as
Jocelyn boldly but unavailingly imposes a single descriptive label,
'the Well-Beloved', on many women in an attempt to impose on
them an identity that will complement him and gratify his desire.
The epigraph for the whole novel 'one shape of many names',
taken from Shelley's 'The Revolt of Islam' (where it is used to
describe the spirit of evil), describes not only Jocelyn's behaviour
but that of the narrators in Hardy's early novels who try to
impose a single ideal of womanliness on all heroines through
their Spencerian generalisations. Like him they fail and, presumably like him also, are now perceived as inimical to the supposed
adored object.

   In the last text the nature of this masculine artistic process
and its inadequacy are highlighted by the extremes to which it
is carried: women are categorised only as being or not being
Jocelyn's Well-Beloved. And though the three Avices are linked
by a common name, (if one ignores the Ann Avice variant), as
women they are particularly distinct from each other in class,
temperament and intelligence. This is very plain with the second
Avice whom Jocelyn, none the less, insists on seeing only as a
'perfect copy' or, ironically transposed into dialect, 'a daps' (*ibid*.
p.97) of her mother. The terms suitable for a sculptor of the
period, such as 'reproducing' and 'copying' are singularly inept
for uncloned human beings; but they serve well as metaphors
for the artifice of the process adopted by Hardy's early narrators
when they attempt to assimilate a range of different individuals
to a standard image of the womanly.

   Such examination of the literary processing of 'uncomplementary'
women is amplified by a detailed picture of the artist at work
on an individual woman. The second Avice is forced to earn her
living as a washerwoman, and this seems to be her description
until Jocelyn sets to work. The narrator satirically translates his
creative process into words:

   It was not the washerwoman that he saw now. In front of her, on
   the surface of her, was shining out that more real, more inter-

penetrating being whom he knew so well! The occupation of the subserving minion, the blemishes of the temporary creature who formed the background, were of the same account in the presentation of the indispensable one as the supporting posts and framework in a pyrotechnic display. (*Ibid*. p.95.)

The process in reverse occurs when he ceases to prefer Nichola Pine-Avon and she becomes an unperson: 'She became a woman of his acquaintance with no distinctive traits; she seemed to grow material, a superficies of flesh and bone merely, a person of lines and surfaces.' Since he no longer writes her as Well-Beloved she is 'a language in living cipher no more' (*ibid*. p.81).

These mismatches between signifier and individual are a spelling out in figurative terms of the mismatch between Cytherea, Elfride, Bathsheba and the web of narratorial generalisations in which they are trapped. In *The Well-Beloved* the resultant need to remodel individuals is further ironised by Jocelyn's plans to dismantle and refurbish the ideal one who has perversely deviated into washerwomanhood: 'he could pack her off to school for two or three years, marry her, enlarge her mind by a little travel, and take his chance of the rest' (*ibid*. p.109).

His attempt and failure to overcome this bit of recalcitrant material mirrors the dialectic present in all Hardy's would-be patriarchal texts. Strikingly Jocelyn comes to the conclusion that the Caros have produced the right 'clay' but not the right 'potter'. But who then is the potter if not himself? From this apparently definitive statement emerges only the idea that moulding women to a preconceived artistic ideal does not work, a conclusion evident to Hardy by 1892.

The same literary process that Jocelyn uses is mirrored by the quotation from Crashaw that is attached as the epigraph to the first part of the novel in the volume edition. It proffers a delicate fantasy in its opening lines:

> Now, if Time knows
> That Her whose radiant brows
> Weave them a garland of my vows;

It deflects into a trap with its close:

Her that dares be
What these lines wish to see:
I seek no further, it is She.

Identification, even as the mere filler of the capitalised feminine pronoun, is evidently the gift of men's words only. Not surprisingly, women's own words which might claim individual identity are revealed, in the kinds of texts represented by Jocelyn's life, as deliberately unheard. Listening to the second Avice through a wall, he is interested only in those cadences of her voice that she shares with the 'real' Avice, her mother: 'The subject of her discourse he cared nothing about . . . He took special pains that in catching her voice he might not comprehend her words. To the tones he had a right, none to the articulations.' (*Ibid*. p.101.) The girl is literally not allowed to mean anything but instead has extracted from her speech only what confirms the Avice/Aphrodite formula. The episode becomes, like others in the text, an account of the entrapment of women in the web of men's language, which is a metonymy for the deletion of women's individuality. Jocelyn characteristically carries out this process by the use of a high-flown philosophical term:

He could not read her individual character, owing to the confusing effect of her likeness to a woman whom he had valued too late. He could not help seeing in her all that he knew of another, and veiling in her all that did not harmonize with his sense of metempsychosis. (*Ibid*. p.96.)

But just as his attempts to capture Aphrodite are 'dusty failures', so too the Caro women are resistant to the imposition of a uniform signification. Their individuality spills out into the corners of the text. In particular the despised second Avice reveals an idiosyncratic attitude to lovers, paralleling Jocelyn's own:

I get tired of my lovers as soon as I get to know them well. What I see in one young man for a while soon leaves him and goes into another yonder, and I follow, and then what I admire fades out of him and springs up somewhere else; and so I follow on, and never fix to one. I have loved *fifteen* a'ready! (*Ibid*. p.107.)

This is, of course, disallowable in a woman and explained away quickly on the basis of a common (and presumably male) ancestor. Jocelyn overlooks it as he does her involvement and, as it turns out, marriage, with another man. Similarly in imposing his tarnished signifier on the third Avice he averts his eyes from the real individual. In *The Pursuit*, in spite of her evident reluctance and the fact that she has a secret lover already, he manages to marry her and to avoid for some time the recognition that her obvious unhappiness is his fault. The marriage is achieved by using Avice's affection for her dying mother who wishes the match. This imposition of inherited tribal identity on an unwilling woman through an appeal to her sense of duty is another exposure of the tyranny of literature (such as Hardy's own early novels) that tries to do the same.

Many times indeed Jocelyn reveals himself to be a literary artist in relation to his own tyrannical acts as he skilfully turns morally undesirable conduct into aesthetically pleasing forms. He is adept at translating his life into themes for literature: his intention of remaking the unsuitable second Avice by schooling and travel blossoms into a subject for a lyric, captured as the idea that she represents his youth which it is an innocent pleasure to recapture. In terms that might make a sonnet he sees himself as offering her not an injury but an 'enriching', which will make a balanced 'reparation' for casting off her mother (*ibid*. p.113). With the third Avice he can erase a sensation of his being 'overmuch selfish' by over-writing it with transforming nostalgia: 'a redeeming quality in the substratum of old pathetic memory by which such love had been created' (*ibid*. p.155). The 'genealogical passion' with which he justifies his hijacking of the unwilling girl forty years his junior is typical poeticising. To liken it to Hardy's own poetry on heredity (Hillis Miller, 1982, pp.168–9), is to miss the satirical point: what is described here is ruthless self-interest ironically seen as rhetorically glossed by its possessor. Such rewritings are not unexpected from a man who describes his domestic strife with Marcia as playing Romeo to her Juliet. And the text finally draws attention to the role of the literary imagination in sustaining appropriating fictions by giving the reader a miniature version of how Jocelyn's vicious tale might be told so as to make a romance:

> Yet to everyone except, perhaps, Avice herself, Jocelyn was the most romantic of lovers. Indeed was there ever such a romance as that man embodied in his relations to her house? Rejecting the first

Avice, the second had rejected him, and to rally to the third with final achievement was an artistic and tender finish to which it was ungrateful in anybody to be blind. (*The Well-Beloved*, p.171.)

This lays bare the literary mechanism that turns a predatory pursuit into a pretty story of a debt of love repaid. Nor is the pursuit seen only as predatory and exacting. Like stories which deal with womanliness and which bypass sexuality, this one denies its existence while in reality privileging it. The text, like those it refers to, is duplicitous. The connection between the statues of Aphrodite and the sculptor's real-life pursuit of the Well-Beloved suggests from the start that the link between them is erotic love. Yet Jocelyn constantly dissociates his passion verbally from the flesh, again with a literary flourish: 'As flesh she dies daily, like the Apostle's corporeal self; because when I grapple with the reality she's no longer in it, so I cannot stick to one incarnation if I would' (*Ibid*. p.65).

He insists that 'nobody but myself has suffered' from his pursuit (*ibid*. p.55). This is technically true since it is made clear that Marcia failed to become pregnant as a result of their liaison: after her departure Jocelyn realises that she must have discovered that 'nothing was likely to happen as a consequence of their elopement' (*ibid*. p.61). Similarly, in the literary folk-tale account of himself that he prepares, but does not use, for Nichola Pine-Avon, he stresses the aphysicality of his passion.

But did she know his history, the curse upon his nature? – That he was the Wandering Jew of the love-world, how restlessly ideal his fantasies were . . . how he was in constant dread lest he should wrong some woman twice as good as himself by seeming to mean what he fain would mean but could not. (*Ibid*. p.77.)

Yet what he sees in all these women is their physical attraction. When the Well-Beloved is embodied in Marcia, the Junoesque: 'She filled every fibre and curve of this woman's form' (*ibid*. p.48). He is struck with a temporary candidate at a party by 'a sky-blue dress, which had nothing between it and the fair skin of her neck, lending her an unusually soft and sylph-like aspect' (*ibid*. p.71). With Nichola herself he notices how her black velvets and silks 'finely set off the exceeding fairness of her neck and shoulders, which, though unwhitened artificially, were without a speck or blemish of the least degree' (*ibid*. p.74). This close scrutiny of her skin has a detail lacking in his subsequent assessment of her intellectual gifts: 'she held also sound rather than current opinions on the plastic arts, and was the first intellectual woman he had seen there that night' (*ibid*. p.74). It is as usual the back not the brain that interests him.

Similarly oblique references to sexual arousal comically underline the nature of the impulse about which he dissimulates even to himself. He is disappointed at a lack of matching sexual 'consciousness' in the second Avice when alone at night with him in his London flat she ingenuously concentrates all her attention on a troublesome mouse. He wants her to recognise 'a danger in their propinquity' (*ibid*. p.128). His own arousal is also implicit in the earlier scene where, after sheltering from a storm by huddling under a boat with Marcia he recognises strong feelings:

> Somewhere about this time . . . he became conscious of a sensation which, in its incipient and unrecognized form, had lurked within him from some unnoticed moment when he was sitting close to his new friend under the lerret. Though a young man, he was too old a hand not to know what this was, and felt alarmed – almost dismayed. (*Ibid*. pp.45–6.)

Since he is busy thinking 'how soft and warm the lady was in her fur covering, as he held her so tightly' the conclusion that this means 'a possible migration of the Well-Beloved' (*ibid*. p.46) becomes an obvious euphemism. This is emphasised by the fact that it is further reflection on her 'fine figure' (*ibid*. p.46) and on the clothes she has discarded for drying at the inn which completes the migration and soon starts the affair (*ibid*. pp.46–7).

In this display of what is not made explicit in the appropriating novels that are being dismantled the meaning of the Avices surname plays a part. It has, like the epigraphs, more significance than at first appears. Caro is, according to Hardy, 'an imitation of a local name . . . this particular modification having been adopted because of its resemblance to the Italian for "dear" ' (*Later Years*, 1930, p.60). It is also, as he fails to point out, not the expected feminine but the masculine form in Italian, and more significantly a Latin word meaning 'flesh'. As the hostile reviewer in *The World* put it: '*Caro, carnis* is the noun with the declension of which Mr. Hardy is perpetually and everlastingly preoccupied in his new book.' (*The World*, 1897, p.13.)

Given this exposure of Jocelyn's art as the rewriting of self-interest, self-deception and the desire for gratification, in more romantic terms, it becomes difficult to see him as a tragic representative of human nature in whose 'experience of disillusionment the once-beloved becomes no longer the sign of a spiritual plenitude, but the sign of an absence' (Hillis Miller, 1982, p.162). Such a reading also overlooks the fact that the medium for the examination of art and the artist in this text is high farce. It is, indeed, to the 'experience of disillusionment' that the third Avice refers when she ingenuously asks whether Jocelyn loved her great-grandmother as well as her mother and grandmother; and to which the narrator laconically harks back when he describes her as 'like her granny . . . too inexperienced to be reserved' (*The Well-Beloved*, p.150). Hillis Miller's very general post-structuralist reading repeats Jocelyn's own literary practice by glossing the plot with the same transforming literary imagination that the latter applies to his own misdeeds. It misses the ironising of the fanciful and artistic idea that women are clay or a medium or an instrument. It still insists on what the Avices mean for Jocelyn, even if that is 'the displacement' of the self's 'love for itself' (Hillis Miller, 1982, p.168); and so repeats the compulsive practice of appropriating women that goes on in the text. If the broad psychoanalytic reading is to stand then the text is about the male psyche to which the Avices minister, not as the combined nanny-Muse that Fowles' account seems to suggest, but as Jocelyn-reflections: 'Only the Avices, because he does not possess them, retain their auras. Jocelyn's refusal to mate with any of the Avices holds off the final revelation of his lack and so keeps him going' (*Ibid*. p.168.)

That there is a lack of fulfilment in the novel is undeniable; that it should be ascribed to 'Jocelyn's refusal to mate with any of the Avices' is baffling. It is in both texts they who resist it (and the two texts are by no means homogeneous): even feminine resistance is here rewritten by Hillis Miller as masculine refusal. Hardy is said to focus, without irony, on 'the male's desire to fulfil himself' (*ibid*. p.167). It is, I think, precisely with irony that the text does so focus, to reveal that the complementary and masculinity-bolstering status assigned to women in patriarchal texts is not sustainable in the face of their individuality, even with heredity to complicate the issue.

In fact, in this double text the implications of the failure to appropriate are spelt out, boldly worked into a huge pattern by the either/or structure of the two plots. In *The Pursuit* the main events of the plot, which can only be seen as a struggle for possession, are as the title suggests initiated by Pearston. He attempts to lead the first Avice into pre-marital relations according to 'Island custom'; presses Marcia into an impulsive marriage; and uses even more coercion to bring about marriage to the reluctant third Avice, already in love with Henri Leverre, Marcia's stepson. In marrying her he commits bigamy: though a common law presumption of a spouse's death after seven years of absence remained until 1938, conditions were attached about determining each case on its own facts. Pearston's 'due enquiries' are desultory as befits a man 'whose pursuits had taught him to regard impressions and sentiments as more cogent than legal rights' (*The Well-Beloved*, serial version, p.741). His magisterial control is evident in his assumption that he can annul the marriage when he discovers Avice's love for Leverre:

> My marriage with Avice is valid if I have a reasonable belief in my first wife's death. Now, what man's belief is fixed, and who shall enter into my mind and say what my belief is at any particular time? The moment I have a reasonable belief that Marcia lives Avice is not my wife . . . (*The Well-Beloved*, serial version, p.774.)

Power lies, in this version, with the man.

In the 'or' half of this *either/or* structure, *The Well-Beloved* where, even in the title, women move centre stage, it is they who dominate the action. Without being asked to, the first Avice makes clear that she will not conform to the Island custom of a trial marriage. This put-down is emphasised rather than concealed by Jocelyn's face-saving pique 'at Avice and her mother's antiquated simplicity in supposing that to be still a grave and operating principle which was a bygone barbarism to himself' (*The Well-Beloved*, p.39). Likewise it is Marcia who, though socially and sexually 'ruined', decrees the end of their affair, preferring scandal to a life-long union 'on the strength of a two or three days' resultless passion' (*ibid*. p.60). The third Avice takes her life into her own hands and elopes before he can complete their marriage. Pierston becomes the object acted upon, until in the last chapter out of pity he marries Marcia (now by a farcical chance confined to a wheelchair for the wedding). With his artistic inspiration also gone, he occupies himself domestically with 'a scheme for the closing of the old natural fountains in the Street of Wells, because of their possible contamination' (*ibid*. p.193). The drying up of erotic and artistic impulses comically imagined here as a mundane job of work has often been noticed: a double impotence concludes what is no longer his story.

What this reversal of gender roles in the alternative plots provides is not an assertion of the superiority of women over men. With its either/or structure the double text offers an interrogation of the conventional power structure, whether men treat women as objects or women treat men as objects. This questioning was implicit in earlier brief transpositions of the sexes such as those referred to in Chapters 3 and 4. The presentation of two equally possible, equally extreme, power structures is a *reductio ad absurdum* of conventional assumptions about a 'natural' hierarchy from which Hardy has moved away. The bold figure takes a stage further the dialectic that emerges in the other novels and gives it lucid form. From the dismantling of the conventional power-structure a further question follows: if neither sex is naturally superior then what are the differences between them, apart from biological ones? To biology, in this text Hardy, as always, gave an over-emphasis, as a reason for women being at a disadvantage. It is said of Mrs Somers (once Nichola Pine-Avon):

> She was another illustration of the rule that succeeding generations of women are seldom marked by cumulative progress, their advance as girls being lost in their recession as matrons . . . And this perhaps not by reason of their faults as individuals, but of their misfortune as child-rearers. (*The Well-Beloved*, p.157.)

On the more general question he arrives at an agnosticism which echoes John Stuart Mill on the subject:

Hence, in regard to that most difficult question, what are the natural differences between the two sexes . . . However great and apparently ineradicable the moral and intellectual differences between men and women might be, the evidence of there being natural differences could only be negative. Those only could be inferred to be natural which could not possibly be artificial – the residuum, after deducting every characteristic of either sex which can admit of being explained from education or external circumstances. (Mill, 1869, p.41.)

Such a position as this which Hardy shares with Mill is already enlightenment. If there is ultimately an absence in this text it is that of a definition conscientiously withheld.

Bibliography

Allen, Grant (1892) 'Fiction and Mrs Grundy', *Novel Review*, 1, pp.294–315.

Allen, Grant (1895) *The Woman Who Did* (John Lane: London and Robert Brothers: Boston).

Auerbach, Nina (1980) 'The Rise of the Fallen Woman', *Nineteenth Century Fiction*, 35, pp.29–52.

Belsey, Catherine (1980) *Critical Practice* (Methuen: London).

Belsey, Catherine (1985) 'Constructing the Subject: Deconstructing the Text', in *Feminist Criticism and Social Change*, Judith Newton and Deborah Rosenfelt (Methuen: New York & London), pp.45–64.

Besant, Walter (1890) 'Candour in English Fiction', *New Review*, 2, pp.6–9. See also Thomas Hardy and Eliza Lynn Linton.

Besant, Walter (1891) 'The Science of Fiction', *New Review*, 4, pp.310–15. See also Thomas Hardy and Paul Bourget.

Björk, Lennart A. (1985) *The Literary Notebooks of Thomas Hardy*, vol. 2 (Macmillan: London & Basingstoke).

Blackwood's Edinburgh Magazine (1858), 83, 'The Condition of Women', pp.139–54.

Boumelha, Penny (1982) *Thomas Hardy and Women: Sexual Ideology and Narrative Form* (Harvester: Brighton).

Boumelha, Penny (1987) 'George Eliot and the End of Realism', in *Women Reading Women's Writing*, ed. Sue Roe (Harvester: Brighton), pp.15–35.

Bourget, Paul (1891) 'The Science of Fiction', *New Review*, 4, pp.304–9. See also Thomas Hardy and Walter Besant.

Braddon, Mary Elizabeth (1862) *Lady Audley's Secret* (Nelson: London).

Braddon, Mary Elizabeth (1864) *The Doctor's Wife* (Simpkin, Marshall, Hamilton, Kent: London).

Brooke, Emma Frances (1894) *A Superfluous Woman* (Heinemann: London).

111

Butler, Lance St J. (1977) see Fowles; for (1989) see Ingham.
Caffyn, Kathleen Mannington (1894) see Iota.
Caird, Mona (1894) *The Daughters of Danaus* (Bliss, Sands, & Foster: London).
Caird, Mona (1897) *The Morality of Marriage* (Redway: London).
Casagrande, Peter J. (1979) 'A New View of Bathsheba Everdene', in *Critical Approaches to the Fiction of Thomas Hardy*, ed. Dale Kramer (Macmillan: London), pp.50–73.
Childers, Mary (1981) 'Thomas Hardy, The Man Who "Liked" Women', *Criticism*, 23 (Fall), pp.317–34.
Coustillas, Pierre (1976) see George Moore.
Cox, Reginald Gordon (1970) *Thomas Hardy: The Critical Heritage* (Barnes & Noble: New York).
Culler, Jonathan (1981) *The Pursuit of Signs* (Routledge & Kegan Paul: London).
Cunningham, Gail (1978) *The New Woman and the Victorian Novel* (Macmillan: London & Basingstoke).
Dowie, Ménie Muriel (1895) *Gallia* (Methuen: London).
Dunne, Mary Chavelita (1893) see Egerton.
Egerton, George (1983) 'Virgin Soil', in *Keynotes and Discords* (Virago: London); *Keynotes* first published by Elkin Mathews & John Lane, 1893, *Discords* first published by the same 1894.
Evans, Robert (1968) 'The Other Eustacia', *Novel*, 1, pp.251–9.
Fawcett, Millicent Garrett (1895) ' "The Woman Who Did" ', *Contemporary Review*, 67, pp.625–31.
Fernando, Lloyd (1967) 'The Radical Ideology of the "New Woman" ', *Contemporary Review* (Adelaide), 2, pp.206–22.
Fernando, Lloyd (1978) *New Women in the Late Victorian Novel* (Pennsylvania State University Press: Pennsylvania).
Fowles, John (1977) 'Hardy and the Hag', in *Thomas Hardy after 50 Years*, ed. Lance St J. Butler (Macmillan: London), pp.28–42.
Frierson, William C. (1968) 'Moore Compromised with the Victorians' in *George Moore's Mind and Art*, ed. Graham Owens (Oliver & Boyd: Edinburgh) pp.45–52.
Gaskell, Elizabeth (1970) *Mary Barton* (Penguin: Harmondsworth).
Goetz, William R. (1983) 'The Felicity and Infelicity of Marriage in *Jude the Obscure*', *Nineteenth Century Fiction*, 38, pp.189–213.
Goode, John (1966) 'Hardy's Sue Bridehead', *Nineteenth Century Fiction*, 20, pp.307–22.
Gorsky, Susan (1973) 'Old Maids and New Women: Alternatives to Marriage in Englishwomen's Fiction', *Journal of Popular Culture*, 7, pp.68–85.
Gosse, Edmund (1891) 'The Science of Criticism', *New Review*, 4, pp.408–11. See also Henry James and Andrew Lang.
Grand, Sarah (1893) *The Heavenly Twins* (Heinemann: London).
Gregor, Ian (1974) *The Great Web: The Form of Hardy's Major Fiction*, (Faber & Faber: London).

Griest, Guinevere L. (1970) *Mudie's Circulating Library and the Victorian Novel* (Indiana State University Press: Bloomington; David & Charles: Newton Abbot, 1971).

Grove, Agnes (1896) 'What Children Should Be Told', *Free Review*, 6, pp.393–9.

Hardy, Florence Emily (1928) *The Early Life of Thomas Hardy: 1840–1891* (Macmillan: London).

Hardy, Florence Emily (1930) *The Later Years of Thomas Hardy: 1892–1928* (Macmillan: London). See also Millgate (1984) for a critical edition of these works.

Hardy, Thomas (1978–1988) *The Collected Letters*, 7 vols, ed. Richard Little Purdy and Michael Millgate (Oxford University Press: Oxford).

Hardy, Thomas, Novels
An Indiscretion in the Life of an Heiress (1976), ed. Terry Coleman (Hutchinson: London).
New Wessex Edition (1975–6) (Macmillan: London):
Desperate Remedies, ed. C.J.P. Beatty; *Under the Greenwood Tree*, ed. Geoffrey Grigson; *A Pair of Blue Eyes*, ed. Ronald Blythe; *Far from the Madding Crowd*, ed. John Bayley; *The Hand of Ethelberta*, ed. Robert Gittings; *The Return of the Native*, ed. Derwent May; *The Trumpet-Major*, ed. Barbara Hardy; *A Laodicean*, ed. Barbara Hardy; *Two on a Tower*, ed. Frank. B. Pinion; *The Mayor of Casterbridge*, ed. Ian Gregor; *The Woodlanders*, ed. David Lodge; *Tess of the d'Urbervilles*, ed. Philip Nicholas Furbank; *Jude the Obscure*, ed. Terry Eagleton; *The Well-Beloved*, ed. Joseph Hillis Miller.
Clarendon Edition (Clarendon Press: Oxford):
The Woodlanders (1981), ed. Dale Kramer (Oxford); *Tess of the d'Urbervilles* (1983), ed. Juliet Grindle and Simon Gatrell (Oxford).
Serial version of *The Well-Beloved*: 'The Pursuit of the Well-Beloved: A Sketch of a Temperament', *Illustrated London News* (1892) 1 October–17 December.
Non-fictional writings, see Harold Orel and Lennart Björk (1985); *Life*, see Florence Emily Hardy (1928) and (1930) and Michael Millgate (1984). 'Candour in English Fiction', *New Review* (1890), 2, 15–21; see also Walter Besant and Eliza Lynn Linton. 'The Science of Fiction', *New Review* (1891), 4, pp.315–19; see also Walter Besant and Paul Bourget. 'The Tree of Knowledge', *New Review* (1894), 10, p.681. 'Laws the Cause of Misery', *Nash's Magazine* (1912), 5, p.669.

Harris, Roy (1983) *Ferdinand de Saussure, Course in General Linguistics* (Duckworth: London).

Harris, Wendell V. (1968) 'John Lane's Keynote Series and the Fiction of the 1890s', *PMLA*, 83, pp.1407–13.

Harris, Wendell V. (1968) 'Egerton: Forgotten Realist', *Victorian Newsletter*, 33, pp.31–5.

Heilman, Robert (1966) 'Hardy's Sue Bridehead', *Nineteenth Century*

Fiction, **20**, pp.307–22.

Helsinger, Elizabeth, K., *et al.* (1983) *The Woman Question*, 3 vols (Manchester University Press: Manchester).

Hillis Miller, Joseph (1982) 'The Compulsion to Stop Repeating', in *Fiction and Repetition: Seven English Novels* (Blackwell: Oxford), pp.147–75.

Hogarth, Janet E. (1895) 'Literary Degenerates', *Fortnightly Review*, **63**, pp.586–98.

Ingham, Patricia, 'Provisional Narratives: Hardy's Final Trilogy', in *Alternative Hardy*, ed. Lance St J. Butler (forthcoming Macmillan: London).

Iota (1894) *A Yellow Aster* (Hutchinson: London).

Jacobus, Mary (1975) 'Sue the Obscure', *Essays in Criticism*, **25**, pp.304–28.

Jacobus, Mary (1978) 'Tess: The Making of a Pure Woman', in *Tearing the Veil: Essays on Femininity*, ed. Susan Lipshitz (Routledge & Kegan Paul: London), pp.77–92.

James, Henry (1888) *Partial Portraits* (Macmillan: London).

James, Henry (1891) 'The Science of Criticism', *New Review*, **4**, pp.398–402. See also Edmund Gosse and Andrew Lang.

Jones, Vivien (1985) *James the Critic* (Macmillan: London & Basingstoke).

Keating, Peter John (1971) *The Working Classes in Victorian Fiction* (Routledge & Kegan Paul: London).

Kozicki, Henry (1974) 'Myths of Redemption in Hardy's *Tess of the d'Urbervilles*', *Papers on Language and Literature*, **10**, pp.150–8.

Kramer, Dale (1979) see Casagrande and Showalter; for *The Woodlanders* (1981) see Thomas Hardy.

Lang, Andrew (1891) 'The Science of Criticism', *New Review*, **4**, pp.403–8. See also Henry James and Edmund Gosse.

Langland, Elizabeth (1980) 'A Perspective of One's Own: Thomas Hardy and the Elusive Sue Bridehead', *Studies in the Novel*, **12**, pp.12–28.

LaValley, Albert J. (1969) *Twentieth Century Interpretations of Tess of the d'Urbervilles* (Prentice Hall: NJ).

Linton, Eliza Lynn (1890) 'Candour in English Fiction', *New Review*, **2**, pp.10–14. See also Thomas Hardy and Walter Besant.

Linton, Eliza Lynn (1868) 'The Girl of The Period', *Saturday Review*, **25**, pp.339–40.

Linton, Eliza Lynn (1883) *The Girl of The Period and Other Social Essays* (Bentley: London).

Lipshitz, Susan, see Mary Jacobus (1978).

Lodge, David (1966) *Language of Fiction: Essays in Criticism and Verbal Analysis of the English Novel* (Routledge & Kegan Paul: London), pp.164–88.

Lucas, John (1977) *The Literature of Change: Studies in the Nineteenth Century Provincial Novel* (Harvester: Hassocks).

McFall, Frances Elizabeth, see Sarah Grand (1893).

Miles, Rosalind (1979) 'The Women of Wessex', in *The Novels of Thomas Hardy*, ed. Anne Smith (Vision: London).

Mill, John Stuart (1869) *The Subjection of Women* (Longmans, Green, Reader, & Dyer: London).

Miller, see Hillis Miller (1982).

Millett, Kate (1970) *Sexual Politics* (Doubleday: NY; Rupert Hart Davis: London, 1971).

Millgate, Michael (1982) *Thomas Hardy: A Biography* (Oxford University Press: Oxford). For *Letters*, see also Thomas Hardy.

Moi, Toril (1985) *Textual/Sexual Politics* (Methuen: London and New York).

Moore, George (1976) *Literature at Nurse or Circulating Morals*, ed. Pierre Coustillas (Harvester: Hassocks).

Newton, Judith and Deborah Rosenfelt, see Catherine Belsey (1985).

Noble, James Ashcroft (1895) 'The Fiction of Sexuality', *Contemporary Review*, **67**, pp.490–8.

North British Review (1850–1), **14**, 'The Social Position of Woman', pp.515–40.

Oliphant, Margaret O.W. (1896) 'The Anti-Marriage League', *Blackwood's Magazine*, **159**, pp.135–49.

Orel, Harold (1967) ed., *Thomas Hardy's Personal Writings* (Macmillan: London).

Owens, Graham (1968) see William C. Frierson.

Page, Norman (1980) see Raymond and Merryn Williams; for (1982) see Merryn Williams.

Poole, Adrian (1981) ' "Men's Words" and Hardy's Women', *Essays in Criticism*, **31**, pp.328–45.

Poovey, Mary (1984) *The Proper Lady and the Woman Writer: Ideology as Style in the Works of Mary Wollstonecraft, Mary Shelley, and Jane Austen* (University of Chicago Press: Chicago & London).

Proust, Marcel (1968) *The Captive*, vol. 10 of *Remembrance of Things Past*, trans. C. K. Scott Moncrieff (Chatto & Windus: London).

Purdy, Richard Little (1968) *Thomas Hardy: A Bibliographical Study* (Clarendon Press: Oxford); first published London 1954. For *Letters*, see also Thomas Hardy.

Roe, Sue (1987) see Boumelha.

Rogers, Kathleen (1975) 'Women in Thomas Hardy', *The Centennial Review*, **19.4** (Fall), pp.249–58.

Rogers, Kathleen (1966) *The Troublesome Helpmate* (University of Washington: Seattle).

Short, Clarice (1958) 'In Defense of *Ethelberta*', *Nineteenth Century Fiction*, **13**, pp.48–57.

Showalter, Elaine (1979) 'The Unmanning of the Mayor of Casterbridge', Dale Kramer ed., *Critical Approaches to the Fiction of Thomas Hardy* (Macmillan: London & Basingstoke), pp.99–115.

Smith, Anne (1979) see Rosalind Miles.

Smith, Sidney (1841) 'Female Education', quoted in *Westminster Review*, **35**, pp.26–7; first published in 1810 in *Edinburgh Review*.

Spencer, Herbert (1897) *The Study of Sociology* (cited from Kegan Paul, Trench, & Trubner: London); first published 1873.

Stead, William Thomas (1894) 'The Novel of the Modern Woman', *Review of Reviews*, **10**, pp.64–74.

Stead, William Thomas (1895) 'The Book of the Month. "The Woman Who Did", by Grant Allen', *Review of Reviews*, **11**, pp.177–90.

Stubbs, Patricia (1979) *Women and Fiction: Feminism and the Novel 1880–1920* (Harvester: Brighton).

Stutfield, Hugh (1895) 'Tommyrotics', *Blackwood's Magazine*, **157**, pp.833–45.

Taylor, Richard H. (1982) *The Neglected Hardy: Thomas Hardy's Lesser Novels* (Macmillan: London & Basingstoke).

Trollope, Anthony (1924) *The Vicar of Bullhampton* (World's Classics, Oxford University Press: Oxford); first published 1870.

Trollope, Anthony (1929) *Ayala's Angel* (1929) (World's Classics, Oxford University Press: Oxford); first published 1881.

Waugh, Arthur (1894) 'Reticence in Literature', *Yellow Book*, **1**, pp.201–19.

Westminster Review (1841) **35** (January–April), 'Woman, her Social Position', pp.24–52.

Williams, Raymond and Merryn Williams (1980) 'Hardy and Social Class', in *Thomas Hardy: the Writer and his Background*, ed. Norman Page (Bell & Hyman: London).

Williams, Merryn (1982) 'Hardy and the "Woman Question" ', in *Thomas Hardy Annual*, **1**, ed. Norman Page (Macmillan: London).

Wittenberg, Judith Bryant (1982) 'Thomas Hardy's First Novel: Women and the Quest for Autonomy', *Colby Library Quarterly*, **18.1** (March), pp.47–54.

World (1897) 24 March: 'Thomas Hardy, Humourist', p.13.

Index